THE FLIGHT OF THE EARLS

LIAM SWORDS

THE
FLIGHT OF
THE EARLS

A Popular History

columba

First published in 2007 by
ᴄhe ᴄoᴌumʙᴀ pʀess
55ᴀ Spruce Avenue, Stillorgan Industrial Park,
Blackrock, Co. Dublin

ISBN 978-1-78218-297-9

Cover design by Helene Pertl | The Columba Press
Book design by Bill Bolger | The Columba Press
Origination by The Columba Press
Printed in Sweden by ScandBook

This hardback edition, 2016

Contents

List of Illustrations   6

Preface: Flight of the Earls   9

Chapter 1: 'A Noble Shipload'   13

Chapter 2: Early Days   22

Chapter 3: The Nine Years War   27

Chapter 4: 'Spanish Ale'   36

Chapter 5: 'A Stormy Passage'   41

Chapter 6: Spanish Flanders   44

Chapter 7: 'A Garden in the very centre of Christendom'   61

Chapter 8: The Devil's Bridge   64

Chapter 9: 'All Roads lead to Rome'   70

Chapter 10: 'Bulls and Benediction'   79

Chapter 11: Last Days   92

List of Illustrations

Facsimile of Ó Cianáin Ms   10
Hugh O'Neill   13
Sir Arthur Chichester   15
Gaelic Banquet, John Derricke, *The Image of Ireland* 1581   16-17
Map: Slane to Rathmullan   18
The O'Donnell Castle, Donegal   25
O'Neill Family Tree and O'Donnell Family Tree   26
Irish infantry or kerne, Derricke   28
The Earl of Essex   29
The Flagship *Ark Royal*   31
Friars blessing Irish chieftains, Derricke   34
Florence Conry. Mural, St Isidore's, Rome   35
O'Neill's submission to Mountjoy   40
Map: Le Havre to Louvain   42
Irish Street, Rome, site of the original Irish College. Photo Liam Swords   47
San Clemente, Rome. Photo Liam Swords   48
St Isidore's, Rome. Photo Liam Swords   48
Luke Wadding. Mural, St Isidore's, Rome   49
Irish Franciscan College of the Immaculate Conception, Prague   51
Collège des Lombards, Paris   51
Dublin Opinion cartoon   52
Irish Regiments of France. Reproduced in R. Hayes, *Irish Swordsmen in France*   55
Scáthán Shacramuinte na h-aithridhe (Louvain 1618), by Aodh MacAingil   58
Anála Ríoghachta Éireann (1630-35)   60
The Duke of Lorraine   62
Lucerne, Switzerland   63
Devil's Bridge (Teufelsbrücke)   65
Conde de Fuentes, Governor of Milan   67
Map: Milan to Rome   72
Pio Nono   74
Scala Santa, Rome. Photo Liam Swords   77
Porto del Populo, Rome. Photo Liam Swords   79
Palazzo Salviati (Hotel Columbus). Photo Liam Swords   80
Pope Paul V   82
Quirinale Palace. Photo Liam Swords   84
San Pietro in Montorio   86
Baron of Dungannon. Portrait, St Isidore's, Rome   92
Tomb of Donough O'Brien in San Stefano Rotundo. Photo Liam Swords   94
Aodh MacAingil. Mural, St Isidore's, Rome   100
Petition to Philip III on behalf of the Irish College, Douai (1608)   102
Tomb of Hugh O'Neill in San Pietro in Montorio. Photo Liam Swords   106

To my sister, Terry, who passed away on the fourth centenary of the Flight.

Preface

Flight of the Earls

IN THE AUTUMN OF 1985 I was assigned by the Irish Episcopal Conference to the Irish College in Paris – where I had previously spent a number of years as an archivist – for the purpose of setting up an Irish chaplaincy. The college, which had been occupied by Polish seminarians since the end of the Second World War, was now entering a new phase with plans for setting up a *Centre Culturel Irlandais* and the bishops wished to continue the religious connection with the college, which had played such a major part in the history of the Irish church. For this reason I resigned from the Radharc television team where I had spent a number of years researching, scripting and sometimes producing some twenty documentaries detailing the Irish connections with Europe. These included the early Irish monks, the Irish Benedictines who formed the Schöttenkloster in Germany, Austria and Switzerland, as well as Malachy of Armagh and Laurence O'Toole, both of whom died in France and whose canonisations were secured by the French in the Middle Ages. Documentaries were also made on many of the Irish Continental Colleges including the two in Lisbon, Saint Patrick's and Corpo Santo, Salamanca, Saint Anthony's in Louvain and Saint Isidore's in Rome, and I also made an earlier documentary with RTÉ on the Irish College in Paris for the commemoration of its fourth centenary in 1978. It was my intention before I left Radharc to make a documentary on the Flight of the Earls and I had completed all the research on the subject.

To prepare for my return to Paris, I bought a French car and took the opportunity of following the path of the Flight from Le Havre to Rome. On this trip I was joined by Dermod McCarthy, a former colleague in Radharc and presently head of the religious department in RTÉ, who, apart from being genial company, was an excellent navigator. We are probably among the very few, if not the only people, who ever undertook this journey.

My other companion on the trip was Tadhg Ó Cianáin in the form of his excellent diary of the Flight. We kept encountering many of the monuments and buildings, still standing today, which he described so accurately in his account, for which I thank Bernadette Cunningham, then librarian in the Mater Dei Library, Clonliffe, who kindly lent me the precious book for the journey. More recently, I have visited every location in Rome where Hugh O'Neill was known to have visited, including Palazzo di Salviati where the Irish fugitives were accommodated.

Facsimile of Ó Cianáin Ms

This book is based mainly on primary sources, such as Ó Cianáin's *Flight of the Earls*, edited and published by Rev. Paul Walsh in 1916, and another version in Irish, published in 1972, *Imeacht na nIarlaí*, with text by Pádraig de Barra and notes by Tomás Ó Fiaich, who was my history professor in Maynooth and inspired my interest in the Irish historical connections with Europe. In fact, he participated as Archbishop of Armagh in some of the Radharc documentaries, travelling with the team and delivering the talks to camera. Also consulted were *Anála Ríoghachta Éireann, Annals of the Four Masters, The Calendar of State Papers, Ireland, James I, 1606-1608*, and *The Calendar of State Papers, Venice, 1607-1615*, as well as 'Miscellanea Vaticano-Hibernica', published in *Archivium Hibernicum*, vol. IV, pp. 247-267. But probably the most important collection of documents, particularly for the last eight years that O'Neill spent in Rome, which were not available to some earlier writers and commentators, were the documents that Micheline Kerney Walsh found, translated and published originally in the *Irish Sword*, vol. 3, pp. 234-244, vol. 5, pp. 224-235, vol. 7, pp. 5-14, no. 26, vol. 7, pp. 136-146, no. 27, vol. 7, pp. 327-337, no. 29, vol. 8, pp. 120-129, no. 31, vol. 8, pp. 230-241, no. 32, vol. 8, pp. 294-203, no. 33, vol. 9, pp. 59-68, no. 34, and vol. 9, pp. 135-136, no. 35, all of which the author had consulted before setting out on his journey. Micheline Kerney Walsh was the daughter of a former Irish envoy to Spain and ideally equipped to work in the Spanish archives. The documents sent by the Irish to Spain were translated from the English original and subsequently retranslated into English by Kerney Walsh. These documents were subsequently published in *'Destruction by Peace' Hugh O'Neill after Kinsale*, in 1986 by Cumann Seanchais Ard Mhacha. Peter Lombard, *The Irish War of Defence 1598-1600*, ed. Matthew J. Byrne (1930), *De Regno Hiberniae*, ed. Patrick F. Moran (1868) were also consulted. While individual quotations are not referenced, it should be easy for the reader to identify the particular source from the above listed primary sources.

Some secondary sources were also consulted, such as 'A Noble Shipload', by Canice Mooney OFM in the *Irish Sword*, vol. 11, pp. 195-203, 'Hugh O'Neill, the Catholic Question and the Papacy', in the *Irish Ecclesiastical Record*, vol. CIV, pp. 65-79, 'The Flight of the Earls', by Nicholas Canny, in *Irish Historical Studies*, vol. 17, pp. 280-39, 'The State of the Realm: English military, political and diplomatic responses to the Flight of the Earls, autumn 1607 to spring 1608', by F. W. Harris, in the *Irish Sword*, vol. 14, pp. 48-65 and 'A house divided: the political community of the lordship of Tír Chonaill and reaction to the Nine Years War', by Darren McGettigan, in *Community in Early Modern Ireland*, eds Robert Armstrong and Tadhg Ó hAnnracháin (2006),

Damien Ó Muirí, 'Dánta Eoghain Ruadh Mhic an Bhaird', in *An Dán Díreach, Léachtaí Cholm Cille* XXIV (1994), John McCavitt, *The Flight of the Earls* (2005).

On other topics surveyed in this work, such as the Irish colleges and the Irish regiments, see Liam Swords, *Soldiers, Scholars, Priests* (1985), *The Green Cockade, The Irish in the French Revolution 1789-1815* (1989), 'History of the Irish College, Paris, 1578-1800', in *Archivium Hibernicum*, XXXV (1980), pp. 3-233, 'Irish Material in the Files of Jean Fromont, Notary, 1703-30, in the Archives Nationales, Paris: Part 1' in *Collectanea Hibernica*, nos 34 and 35, pp. 77-115, and Part 2, 36-37, pp. 85-139, Micheline Kerney Walsh, 'Irish Soldiers and the Irish College in Paris 1706-1771,' in Liam Swords, ed., *The Irish-French Connection, 1578-1978*, pp. 63-87; also in the same work see, Cathaldus Giblin OFM, 'The Irish Colleges on the Continent', pp. 9-20, and Swords, 'Collège des Lombards', pp. 44-62, 'The Irish in Paris at the end of the *ancien régime*' in O'Connor, Thomas, *The Irish in Europe 1580-1815*, pp. 191-205, and in the same work, see also, Patricia O'Connell, 'The early-modern Irish college network in Iberia, 1590-1800', pp. 49-64, Éamon Ó Cíosáin, 'A hundred years of Irish migration to France, 1590-1688', pp. 93-106, Edward Corp, 'The Irish at the Jacobite court of Saint-Germain-en-Laye, pp. 143-156, Priscilla O'Connor, 'Irish clerics and Jacobites in early eighteenth-century, 1700-30', pp. 175-190.

I would like to thank Luke Dempsey OP and Paul Murray OP who encouraged me to undertake this work on a recent trip to the Convitto S. Tommaso, the original Irish College in via degli Ibernesi, Rome; Fintan Duffy and Mary Ann Bolger, who reunited me with my original research material from which I had become separated; Brenda and Mike Kirby; Máirtín Mac Niocláis, who gave me access to his Irish collection and guided me through it. My thanks are due to the staff of *Biblioteca Apostolica Vaticana*, to Trish Quigley, Áine Stack, Anne O'Carroll, Mary Perrem and Mary Glennon of the Milltown Institute library, as well as to Louis Brennan OFM of St Isidore's, Rome, and Mícheál Mac Craith, Ollscoil na hÉireann, Gaillimh. A special word of thanks is due to my publisher Seán O Boyle and designer, Bill Bolger, whose close friendship I treasure far more than their widely recognised expertise.

Chapter One

'A Noble Shipload'

'THAT WAS A NOBLE SHIPLOAD, for it is certain that in modern times the sea has not poured forth from Ireland nor the wind wafted a shipload that would have proved finer or more illustrious, or nobler on grounds of ancestry, or better for deeds or bounty, valour and exploits, than they, had God permitted them to remain in their country till their children attained manhood.'

Thus the *Annals of the Four Masters* described what was later called the Flight of the Earls, one of the most significant and dramatic incidents in modern Irish history, which continues to have reverberations to this day on the island of Ireland. In the immediate aftermath of the Flight, the plantation of Ulster was set in motion, dispossessing the native Irish and replacing them with colonists largely of Scottish and Presbyterian origins, giving rise to a bitter sectarian divide in the province, which still remains after four hundred years.

On Friday, 14 September 1607, Hugh O'Neill, Earl of Tyrone, Rory O'Donnell, Earl of Tyrconnell and Cuchonnacht Maguire, Lord of Fermanagh, with their families and followers, took ship at Rathmullan in County Donegal and set sail from Lough Swilly for La Coruña in north-western Spain. In all there were ninety-nine persons on board, including a group of secular priests, Franciscan friars and young students. Among the women pas-

Hugh O'Neill

sengers were O'Neill's fourth wife, Countess Catherine Magennis, Nuala O'Donnell, sister of Rory and Caffar, and the latter's wife Rose O'Dogherty. Nuala O'Donnell had left her husband Niall Garbh O'Donnell when he offered his services to the English in autumn 1600. O'Neill had three sons by Catherine, two of whom he took with him, John, the eldest and the youngest, Brian, who was then about three years old. Five-year-old Conn was at fosterage and could not be found and was left behind. The youngest passenger was Rory O'Donnell's son, Hugh, who was not yet a year old and was looked after by nurses as his mother, Bridget Fitzgerald, was at her family home in Maynooth and prevented by circumstances from joining her husband. The other child on board, also called Hugh, was the two-year-old son of Caffar and Rose.

Ten days earlier, on 4 September, a ship from France had arrived in Lough Swilly. The master of the ship was John Rath from Drogheda who had been sent by O'Neill to Spain about six months earlier to seek the King's assistance. Three others arrived with him in Lough Swilly, Cuchonnacht Maguire, Matthew Tully and Donough O'Brien.

Cuchonnacht Maguire, Lord of Fermanagh was described by the Four Masters as 'endowed with wisdom and beauty of person' who could disguise himself so well that his closest friends could barely recognise him. It was probably about him that the story was recounted that a guest at a banquet queried why he did not sit at the head of the table. 'Where Maguire sits,' he replied, 'is the head of the table.' According to the English ambassador in Brussels, when Maguire heard of O'Neill's summons to London, he went to Brittany where, disguising himself as a merchant, he hired a ship at Nantes with some fishing nets to give the impression he was going to fish off the coast of Ireland. He brought the ship to Dunkirk from where he sailed to Ireland.

Matthew Tully was O'Neill's official representative at the Spanish court. He had spent many years in France and Spain where he had acquired a fluency in these languages. Donough O'Brien from Clare, a cousin of the Earl of Thomond, had also spent a long time on the Continent where he first went as a child.

O'Brien landed at night and went straight to the Earl of Tyrconnell

Cuchonnacht
Maguire

to inform him of the ship's arrival and he immediately sent the Franciscan, Owen Groome Magrath, with
the message for O'Neill which he received at Slane on
6 September. He was there to meet Sir Arthur Chichester, the Viceroy of Ireland, to discuss the summons
he had received to go to England. King James had
written to Chichester in July ordering that O'Neill
present himself in London in late September or in
the beginning of October. Chichester remarked that
when O'Neill got the King's summons, 'He did lose
his former cheerfulness and grew often exceeding

pensive.' And he had very good reason to be so. As he later informed the
King of Spain, 'The king of England summoned us to London with the
intention of either beheading us or putting us in the Tower of London
for life.'

Sir Arthur
Chichester

After two days, he left Slane and spent the night of 8 September in
Mellifont in the house of Garret Moore. Mellifont Abbey had been
granted to Moore's father in 1566 and remained the seat of the family
until the eighteenth century. Mellifont was the first Cistercian Abbey to
be founded in Ireland, in 1142. It followed a visit from St Malachy of
Armagh, on his way to Rome, to St Bernard at his famous monastery at
Clairvaux where he placed four of his Irish companions to be trained in
the Cistercian rule.

Slane to
Rathmullan
6–16 Sept.
1607

Despite the fact that Garret Moore had served with the English during
the Nine Years War against O'Neill, they remained on friendly terms and
O'Neill placed his eldest son, John, by Catherine Maginnis, to be educated with Moore's family. Untypically, he 'wept abundantly when he took
his leave, giving a solemn farewell to every child and every servant in the
house, because it was not his manner to use such compliments'. When
he left on Sunday, he took the little boy with him, which Garret duly
reported to Chichester, making the latter 'suspect he had some mischief
in his head', though he never suspected 'his flight beyond the seas'.

O'Neill continued his journey, passing through Dundalk, Armagh
and Dungannon until he finally reached one of his habitations near
Stewartstown where he remained for two nights. It was probably here

Gaelic Banquet.
John Derricke,
*The Image of
Ireland* 1581

A   Now when into their fenced holdes, the knaues are entred in
       To smite and knocke the cattell downe, the hangmen doe be
       One plucketh off the Oxes cote, which he euen now did wea
       Anothe r lacking pannes, to boyle the flesh, his hide prepare.
C   These theeues attend vpon the fire, for seruing vp the feast:
B   And Fryer smelfeast sneaking in, doth preace amongst the b

3

D

Who play'th in Romish toyes the Ape, by counterfetting Paull:
For which they doe award him then, the highest roome of all.
Who being set, because the cheere, is deemed little worth:
Except the same be intermitt, and lac'de with Irish myrth.
Both Barde, and Harper, is preparde, which by their cunning art,
Doe strike and cheare vp all the gestes, with comfort at the hart.

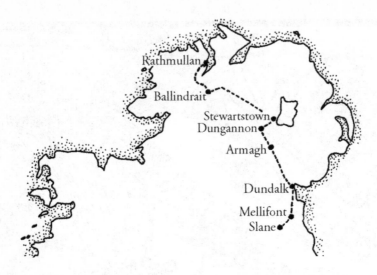

that he collected his wife, Catherine and his youngest son, three-year-old Brian, and other members of his household. They travelled all night across the Sperrin mountains which apparently took a lot out of Catherine. She slipped down off her horse and told her husband in tears that she could go no further. O'Neill was not prepared to humour her. He 'drew his sword and swore a great oath that he would kill her in the place, if she would not pass on with him', and added for good measure, 'and put on a more cheerful countenance withal'. Catherine's distress may have been caused by the fact that her second eldest son, five-year-old Conn, was not with them and there was almost no hope that he would be found in time, as he was in fosterage with a family who were almost nomadic, following their herds in search of pasturage 'after the manner of the Tartars'. Several attempts were made afterwards to rescue him and bring him to the Netherlands but without success.

At midday they arrived at Caffar O'Donnell's home in Ballindrait and that night they set out again, accompanied by Caffar and his wife, Rose O'Dogherty, and other members of their household. As before, they were obliged to travel under cover of darkness lest they be spotted by passersby who were more than willing to keep the English informed. O'Neill claimed that there were 'so many eyes watching over him as he could not drink a full carouse of sack (white wine) but the state was advertised thereof within a few hours after'. Five miles below Strabane they crossed the river Foyle and reached Rathmullan at daybreak on Friday 14 September, where they found Rory, Earl of Tyrconnell, Maguire, with many of his followers, loading the ship with stores of food and drink.

At about midday on Friday, 14 September 1607, the passengers, to the number of ninety-nine, boarded the ship, and set sail for La Coruña in Spain. There were eight O'Neills including Hugh's son, Hugh, the Baron of Dungannon, as well as five O'Hagans, two Kennys, two O'Mahons and two O'Loughrans. There were also members of Old English families whom O'Neill had befriended, such as Richard Weston from Dundalk, Christopher Plunkett, George Moore, Peter Preston, Patrick Rath, John Rath and George Cashel. There were also a number of priests including O'Neill's own chaplain and that of his wife, as well as thirteen other priests and twelve students who wished to study in Flanders. One of the priests, the Franciscan, Maurice Donleavy, who accompanied O'Donnell, became the Irish provincial. A Spanish survivor of the Armada, Pedro Blanco, who had been rescued by O'Neill in 1588 and had remained with him ever since, also travelled.

Those who travelled with Rory O'Donnell included Hugh, Caffar's son, who was about two years old. It was said that he had six toes and it was prophesied that when such a child would be born to the O'Donnell family, 'He shall drive all the Englishmen out of Ireland.' There were also eight of the Gallagher family, which had close association with the O'Donnells, and two McDavitts. Cuchonnacht Maguire was accompanied by two gentlemen and two servants.

A number of servants accompanied O'Neill, including two ladies-in-waiting for the Countess Catherine, as well as three maids, three pages and number of manservants as well as seven other servants. The O'Donnells had eighteen servants, including two nurses for the young Baron of Donegal, four for Nuala, a lady-in-waiting, a maid and two pages.

Behind them the fugitives left several broken families. Rory O'Donnell's wife, Bridget Fitzgerald, was visiting her family in Maynooth and the seventeen-and-a-half-year-old was then expecting their second child. Rory sent a priest to fetch her but by the time he reached her the boat had already left. Another boat was procured, but Bridget declined the offer, probably through pressure from her family.

Passengers

Broken families

The Kildare Geraldines were then in league with the Dublin government against O'Neill, and Bridget's own father had been killed on expedition to Tyrone in 1597.'

Caffar O'Donnell and Rose O'Dogherty left their young son, Conn, behind and he was later seized on the orders of Chichester. Nuala O'Donnell shed no tears for Niall Garbh, whom she had already left, but she must have shed bitter tears for her son, Neachtan, whom she left behind.

Some of the followers of O'Neill and O'Donnell also left families behind: Henry O'Hagan left a wife and children; Murtagh Kenny, a wife; Richard Weston left his wife, Máiréad, and his son, Richard, in Dundalk. Tadhg Ó Cianáin, who kept a diary recording a daily account of the Flight, belonged to a literary family who chronicled the Maguires for a few hundred years and the obituaries of several of his ancestors are recorded in the Irish annals. He himself left behind a wife and children. Sean Crone McDavitt left a wife and children in Buncrana but he never forgot them. After spending seven years in Rome, he travelled for five months until he reached Bordeaux. There he found a ship's captain who undertook to deliver a letter to his wife, Finola O'Doherty, in Buncrana, begging her 'to come with speed ... and bring the rest of our children at once with yourself.' He was prepared to send her thirty pounds to cover her expenses. The letter was seized by Chichester who thought McDavitt's wife could 'do no harm on the other side of the sea' while in Ireland she could act as a spy. In fact, he recommended that she and the other children and wives of fugitives should be sent to join their husbands, making them more burdensome for those who received and supported them. It is not known if Finola and her children ever rejoined her husband.

The Flight of the Earls presented the government with just the pretext they needed to further their plans for Ulster. That December the Earls were 'attainted by outlawry' and adjudged to have forfeited their lands to the crown. Plans were drawn up to colonise Ulster and they were completed in 1610 with the establishment of the Plantation of Ulster. The Earls would have plenty of time in exile, particularly Hugh O'Neill, to reflect on the events which led them to take this momentous decision to leave Ireland. It appears that Rory O'Donnell had jumped the gun because he had lost a considerable amount of his territory and power since the settlement and he was not able to withstand Niall Garbh who was aspiring, with English backing, to be The O'Donnell. And Maguire's position in Fermanagh was even worse. For both of these the prospect of a military career on the Continent was far more attractive than the fate that awaited them in Ulster. On the other hand, O'Neill had retained most of his earldom and the English administration were inclined to indulge him somewhat. But the decision was taken out of his hands by the sudden arrival of the ship. If he did not go, the English would assume that he remained behind to organise a rebellion while the others had gone to get Spanish help.

It would probably be of little consolation for him to have known that the English conquest of Ireland was inevitable and irreversible. The clash between Gaelic tribalism, ridden with its internecine rivalries, and a unified English bureaucratic machine, backed by superior military power, would prove to be a mis-match of enormous proportions. O'Neill's decision to flee the country at most only accelerated that process. However, little did the fugitives suspect that they would never again return to Ulster and that that province would be ridden with deep sectarian division which still, after four hundred years, continues to defy the best efforts of the British and Irish governments to effect a reconciliation between the two communities. Some further exploration of the events leading up to the flight is needed to clarify O'Neill's final decision.

Chapter Two

Early Days

WHEN HUGH O'NEILL returned to Ulster as Baron of Dungannon in 1568 he could reasonably have anticipated advancing, with full English backing, to the Earldom of Tyrone, first granted to his grandfather, Conn Bacach O'Neill, in October 1482. This resulted from a new policy adopted by the English which came to be known as 'surrender and regrant'. Irish chiefs were persuaded to surrender their lands to the Crown and they were then regranted to them to be held by titles valid in English law. In the north, Manus O'Donnell was the first to submit and he was followed six months later by Conn Bacach O'Neill, who was the first O'Neill ever to visit the English court, prostrate himself before the King and be confirmed with the title, Earl of Tyrone. These submissions were to have far-reaching consequences and, as the Four Masters later remarked, 'the sovereignty of every Gaelic lord was lowered'. This new system was based on succession by primogeniture, while the Gaelic system was based on election within the upper echelons of the clan.

Conn Bacach O'Neill

Hugh was just eighteen years of age when he returned from England where he had spent nearly eight-and-a-half years. Youths matured quickly in those days. Henry VIII was married at that age. Hugh's uncle, Shane the Proud, was already fighting for his rights in Ulster, almost as soon as he left his teens and by 1599 he was acknowledged as The O'Neill on the death of Conn Bacach. That year, at the age of nine,

Hugh O'Neill

Hugh was taken to England by Sir Henry Sidney, when he completed his first term as Lord Deputy of Ireland, with the intention of grooming the young lad to play an important role in the English administration of his ancestral lands in Ulster.

 At that age it is difficult to estimate how much Hugh was aware of his own murky background. His father, Matthew, was Conn's eldest son and named Baron of Dungannon in 1542. Matthew's brother, Shane, claimed that he was the eldest legitimate son, alleging that Matthew was the son of Alison Kelly, the wife of a Dundalk blacksmith and Matthew's real father. Bitter war ensued between the two rivals, leading to the murder of Matthew and his eldest son, Brian, four years later, leaving Hugh heir to the earldom. The cruelty and viciousness of Gaelic chiefs could only be matched by that of modern drug-barons against those who muscled onto their patch, except that, in the case of the former, it was usually against their own kith and kin. Hugh O'Neill himself was said to have hanged a rival, Hugh Gavelock McShane O'Neill, with his own hands.

Hugh's Ulster childhood was probably best described by his biographer, Sean O'Faolain: 'The child Hugh, therefore, grew up at Dungannon in an atmosphere of raid and counter-raid, bloodshed and danger, bitter argument, divided loyalties. As soon as he could absorb anything, he drank in through his very pores the lesson of his murdered father, his murderous, rebellious uncle Sean ...; he absorbed the highly pertinent lesson of his murdered brother, of the whispers about his father's origins and his own, and behind it all the two essential lessons ... the value of power and the great power of England.'

Elizabethan England was a far cry from O'Neill's old Gaelic Ulster. When his uncle, Shane the Proud, visited the court of Queen Elizabeth, the courtiers looked at him 'with as much wonderment as if he had come from China or America' with his escort of long-haired gallowglasses, armed with battle-axes, with their bright saffron shirts and their flowing sleeves and short tunics beneath furry cloaks. In fact the comparison with native Americans was not very far wide of the mark. Unlike the English, both were rural peoples following a pastoral life, living in encampments and roaming the plains with their buffalo or cattle, in search of pastures. The only significant difference was that the better sort of Gaelic society was mounted while the native Americans had to wait for some time after the Spanish *conquistadores* had introduced horses into their continent before they followed suit.

Hugh was taken to Sidney's great castle at Ludlow in Shropshire as Sidney had been made Lord President of Wales the year before and resided there in his great keep on the tributary of the Severn. He was brought up in the new religion, Protestantism, with 'a Puritanism that was always solemn and earnest, and sometimes hard and narrow'. He spent time too with the Queen's favourite, Robert Dudley, Earl of Leicester, in Norfolk and later referred to him as 'my honourable patron who from my youth had a special care of my bringing up and well-doing'. In the early years after his return to Dungannon, Hugh stuck close to the English, whom he believed would best help him to realise his ambitions. He was rewarded in 1587 when he was promoted to the Earldom and was granted larger territories than any other Earl in Ireland, including the south-eastern part of Tyrone and a large part of County Armagh. That year he attended the parliament in Dublin, taking his seat in the upper house.

Red Hugh O'Donnell

Elsewhere in the province, discontent with England was growing. Red Hugh O'Donnell, at the age of sixteen, was seized by trickery in 1587 with other hostages. A sea-captain called Skinner was picked up on the quays in Dublin and persuaded with bribes and threats to sail to Donegal with a party of soldiers and a generous supply of sack or white wine. He arrived in Lough Swilly and anchored close to Rathmullan castle, posing as a trader newly arrived from Spain. Young O'Donnell was enticed aboard, presumably without any great difficulty, and after a few hours savouring the wine, he was in no condition to notice that the ship had lifted sail and was on its way to Dublin where he was to spend over three years a prisoner in the Castle. When he escaped in 1592 he returned to Tyrconnell where he was inaugurated as The O'Donnell while O'Neill became The O'Neill in June 1593.

The Earl of Tyrone was now in effective control of the more impor-tant part of the O'Neill lordship and the greatest of the Irish lords, though his acceptance of the title 'The O'Neill' was not necessarily a declaration of war against the queen. Both O'Neill and O'Donnell were war-lords, exerting hegemony and exacting tribute in cattle, often with great brutality, over a sizeable number of lesser chiefs. O'Donnell's sphere of influence extended all the way down to Lower Connacht where his minions included O'Connor Sligo, the O'Haras, the O'Harts, the O'Dowds, the McDonaghs and the Burkes. Between them the two Earls controlled a large part of the north and west of Ireland.

The O'Donnell Castle, Donegal

The alliance between the two men was cemented by intermarriage. O'Neill had married Siobhán, Red Hugh's sister, who bore him two sons, Hugh and Henry, before her death in 1591. Red Hugh himself, at the age of nineteen in 1592 married Rose, a daughter of O'Neill born outside marriage, though this marriage later failed because of her illegitimacy and her failure to produce children.

As elsewhere in Europe, marriages were not affairs of the heart but intended as inter-family alliances and because they only took place within the same ruling class there was a limited number of suitable women to chose from. For whatever other marriage needs had to be met, there was a fairly extensive pool of women more than happy to share a bed with an O'Neill or O'Donnell. The *droit du seigneur* was just as widely practised in Gaelic Ireland as elsewhere in Europe.

Hugh O'Neill eloped with Mabel Bagenal, sister of Marshal Henry Bagenal, commander of the Queen's army in Ireland, and married her in 1591 in a Protestant ceremony performed by the Bishop of Meath. He was then forty-one and she was merely twenty, but women married early at that time, and men early and often. She soon got over her infatuation and left him when she discovered he had two mistresses already installed or, as O'Neill himself put it, 'I affected two other gentlewomen.' His uncle, Shane O'Neill, was believed to have had swarms of children by such women and was never known to have denied his parentage to any of them. The offspring of these liaisons were generally acknowledged in some form which enhanced the status of their families.

O'Neill Family Tree

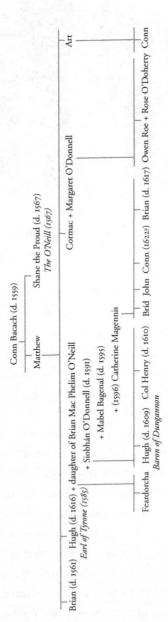

Conn Bacach (d. 1559)

Matthew   Shane the Proud (d. 1567) *The O'Neill (1567)*   Cormac + Margaret O'Donnell   Art

Brian (d. 1561)   Hugh (d. 1616) + daughter of Brian Mac Phelim O'Neill *Earl of Tyrone (1585)*
+ Siobhán O'Donnell (d. 1591)
+ Mabel Bagenal (d. 1595)
+ (1596) Catherine Magennis

Feardorcha   Hugh (d. 1609)   Col Henry (d. 1610)   Bríd   John   Conn (1622?)   Brian (d. 1617)   Owen Roe + Rose O'Doherty   Conn
Baron of Dungannon

O'Donnell Family Tree

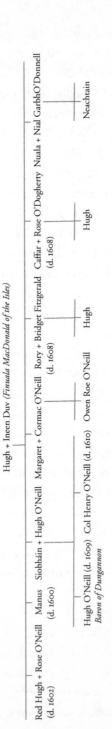

Hugh + Ineen Duv *(Finuala MacDonald of the Isles)*

Red Hugh + Rose O'Neill   Manus   Siobháin + Hugh O'Neill   Margaret + Cormac O'Neill   Rory + Bridget Fitzgerald   Caffar + Rose O'Dogherty   Nuala + Nial Garbh O'Donnell
(d. 1602)   (d. 1600)   (d. 1608)   (d. 1608)

Hugh O'Neill (d. 1609)   Col Henry O'Neill (d. 1610)   Owen Roe O'Neill   Hugh   Hugh   Hugh   Neachtain
Baron of Dungannon

Chapter Three

The Nine Years War

THE ENGLISH continued to encroach on O'Neill's neighbours and allies in Ulster. Hugh Maguire, his nephew-in-law, was forced into rebellion in 1594 to protect his interests and was helped by his cousin, Red Hugh. O'Neill himself kept his powder dry and continued his policy of remaining compliant to the Queen, even to the point of assisting Bagenal against Maguire, but at the same time he began making preparations for quite a different scenario. He bought arms and ammunition in Scotland and together with O'Donnell he recruited Scots mercenaries from there. Red Hugh's mother, Iníon Dubh, who was originally Fionnuala McDonald from the Isles, played a major role in these transactions.

The real struggle began in 1595. In February O'Neill sent his brother to capture and destroy the fort and bridge that Essex had built over the river Blackwater. In summer he attacked and defeated at Clontibret, close to Monaghan, a large force under Bagenal. In June he was proclaimed a traitor. That September O'Neill and O'Donnell wrote to Philip II looking for help and he sent, the following year, a ship with arms and ammunition.

O'Neill and O'Donnell employed guerilla tactics in their war against the crown forces, which was admirably suited to the terrain in Ulster with which they were very familiar and could exploit to maximum advantage. A contemporary remarked: 'It was impossible to come to a

Irish infantry
or kerne,
Derricke

pitched battle with the Irish, whose habit is to strike and then fly into the dense forests where they are safe.' This was typified by the battle of the Yellow Ford in 1598. The English had garrisoned a fort on the river Blackwater, within sight of the cathedral city of Armagh, and O'Neill promptly blockaded it. Soon the garrison there was starving and Bagenal, with a force of 4,000 men, was sent to relieve it. On the march he was continually harassed by Red Hugh and Maguire and eventually defeated on 14 August, with the loss of nearly half his force and his own life.

The battle had a huge impact on the rest of the country, causing a virtual collapse of English authority in Connacht, Munster and even parts of Leinster. Red Hugh had total mastery in the greater part of Connacht. In Munster scattered settlers fled in fear and sought shelter in Cork, Waterford, Limerick and other towns. Philip II was then danger-ously ill in his palace of the Escorial and died a short time later on 13 September. There was some doubt whether Philip III would be as sup-portive of O'Neill, as he had other preoccupations which took precedence with him. When the Pope heard of the victory at Clontibret he ordered the guns of Castel Sant' Angelo to be discharged and a *Te Deum* was sung in St Peter's. Early the following year, he issued a brief, granting to all those who joined 'the Catholic army' the same indulgences once granted to the Crusaders, and later he sent a letter to O'Neill congratul-ating him on the establishment of 'a holy league' with which with the help of the 'Lord of Hosts you have on divers occasions been successful against the English – those apostates from the Church and the Faith'.

At this juncture, 1599, Robert Devereux, Earl of Essex, and the Queen's favourite, was sent to Ireland as Lord Lieutenant. He was the son of the first Earl of Essex who had befriended O'Neill when he was a youth in England. He spent twenty-one weeks achieving virtually nothing, except subduing Leinster and parts of Munster. The Queen's patience was running thin and she peremptorily ordered him to move north-ward. Essex sent Sir Henry Wotton to negotiate a suspension of arms with O'Neill. He spent a day with O'Neill and his army, which he claimed numbered 25,000. He considered O'Neill 'as cunning and suspicious as you could meet'. Wotton later became English ambassador to Venice and one of the princi-pal reporters in Europe on the Flight.

Essex margin note: Essex

The Earl of Essex

Essex himself advanced with 4,000 men but was confronted by O'Neill just south of Carrickmacross. O'Neill persuaded him to parley and the pair conversed privately for the best part of an hour, with O'Neill on horseback in a river while Essex stood on the bank. What passed between them is un-known but the result was an agreed cessation of hostilities. Queen Elizabeth was furious with Essex when she heard what had happened: 'To trust this traitor on his oath is to trust the devil upon religion.'

Later, there were rumours of a conspiracy being hatched between them and there were some credible subscribers to the notion of this conspiracy. The Spanish Franciscan, Matthew de Oviedo, who was later named Archbishop of Dublin, informed Philip III in April 1600 'that O'Neill had almost prevailed upon the Earl of Essex to desert the Queen's cause and join that of Your Majesty and surrender all the Realm to you.' Bishop Eoghan O'Hart of Achonry, who attended and spoke at the Council of Trent, told a Munster visitor in March 1601 that he had recently attended a parley held in Sligo by Red Hugh who showed him a letter from Essex to O'Neill stating 'that he would shortly draw the English forces from Ireland into England ... and desired O'Neill to send him a thousand light men to play withal in England.' Whatever the truth was, Essex suddenly left Ireland and returned to England against Elizabeth's express wishes. He was later imprisoned and beheaded in February 1601. At his trial for treason in 1601 it was alleged that Tyrone had urged him 'to stand for himself' promising that if he did 'he would join with him'. Red Hugh was at Donegal Abbey at Easter 1601 when he first heard the news that Essex 'had lost his head, for which they all seemed to be very sorrowful'.

The man who succeeded Essex in February 1600 was a completely different kettle of fish, as O'Neill would very soon learn to his cost. Charles Blount, Lord Mountjoy, was a soldier and administrator. He sought to maintain pressure on Tyrone and his allies all the year round and not just during short summer campaigns, as had been the custom of his predecessors up to now.

O'Neill and O'Donnell had constantly to watch their backs. O'Faolain expresses it well: 'In his life Tyrone was not broken by England but by Ireland; by its deep atavism and inbreeding, so characteristic of abortive and arrested cultures in all ages of the world's history.' One setback and they would be deserted by their so-called allies in droves. O'Faolain gives a perceptive analysis of what he calls 'the crazily chaotic Irish system. These men failed Tyrone, not from any natural bent toward treachery but because they had been made incapable by centuries of anarchy, of bringing this incipient unity to any effective, continuous, well-timed action … they were victims of a tradition and a system that had by the sixteenth century become quite unworkable, and corrupted all who attempted to live by it.' The most striking example of this was the behaviour of Red Hugh's own brother-in-law and second cousin, Niall Garbh O'Donnell. Mountjoy encouraged Niall Garbh to claim Tyrconnell over the head of the existing chieftain, Red Hugh, with the result that Niall entered the war on the English side, personally killing Red Hugh's brother, Manus, in 1600. He took Ballyshannon and occupied in August 1601 Donegal Abbey where there were some forty Franciscan friars, but Red Hugh could do nothing as he was otherwise pressingly engaged. News had come that the long-awaited Spanish help had finally arrived.

From as far back as 1595, Hugh O'Neill was in communication with Philip II, from whom he sought military assistance to the tune of 3,000 men, and offered him the crown of Ireland if he would deliver them from the English intruders. The one time Gaelic war-lord assumed the role of

The Flagship
Ark Royal

 The greatest flotilla ever launched on the high seas was assembled at La Coruña, consisting of 130 ships, led by a fighting core of 12 galleons and carrying 30,000 men.

The appearance of the Armada off the English coast caused widespread panic. On 5 August a great storm blew up, hurling the flotilla up the North Sea, past Scotland and down round the coast of Ireland. The impact of the Armada on Ireland was slight, leaving a number of castaways washed up on the coast who were for the most part badly treated except in Ulster and north Connacht. The Earl of Tyrone was one of the very few who helped the survivors, which first made Dublin ministers question his loyalty. Some of them remained on in his service and were killed in the battles he fought. One of them, Pedro Blanco, remained with him for almost twenty years and later accompanied him on the Flight. Why O'Neill did so, it is impossible to know as it was so much out of character. He even went so far as to rebuke O'Donnell, who bartered forty of the castaways to secure the release of his son, Red Hugh, from Dublin Castle.

Elsewhere they received no quarter from the native Irish. Those cast away off Clare Island were ruthlessly murdered as they limped ashore by the followers of the O'Malleys. One estimate put at 3,000 the number of those who managed to swim to land and who were slain. Many of those were slaughtered by the English settlers. Richard Bingham claimed that his brother, George, executed seven or eight hundred, which might explain why Ballymote Castle was burnt in October 1588 by the O'Connors, O'Harts and O'Dowds 'who called themselves the Pope's and King Philip's men'. The Spaniards were expected then to arrive in Sligo in five days and there was an 'expectation of a general revolt'. Three hundred were formally executed in Galway city.

patriot *malgré lui*. His overtures to Spain were England's greatest nightmare. Ever since the Great Armada was launched in July 1588, the Spanish threat continued to hang over England, where it was quickly realised that Ireland could provide the bridgehead needed to make that threat a reality.

As news of the fate of the Great Armada percolated back to Spain, Philip II, entombed in his monastery palace of Escorial, sank into deep depression, spending long hours in prayer, closeted only with his confessor. A son of the Emperor Charles V and grandson of Ferdinand and

Isabella, whose marriage led to the creation of Spain as a nation, 'His Most Catholic Majesty' was the self-appointed champion of the Counter-Reformation and the implacable enemy of heretics everywhere. He had been briefly married to Mary Tudor, known to later generations of English as 'Bloody Mary' because of her harsh treatment of Protestants. She was the daughter of Henry VIII and his first wife, Catherine of Arragon, but it was a childless and loveless union which ceased at her death in 1558. The Armada represented an enormous setback to his dream to re-unite Christendom. It was to this man that Hugh O'Neill had turned for help.

O'Neill was even less likely a Counter-Reformation figure than an Irish nationalist, but he was a sufficiently able politician or actor to play either or both roles, whichever would serve his own interests best. Here was a man who was raised in his formative years as a Protestant, who sought out a Protestant bishop to perform his third marriage, to Mabel Bagenal, who had one of his sons educated with a Protestant family and who supported, if not admired, the notorious Myler McGrath, who abandoned his Franciscan habit for a Protestant mitre, acquiring the archbishopric of Cashel, together with a few minor bishoprics.

There is some evidence to suggest that Red Hugh O'Donnell's religious credentials were somewhat better. He was very closely associated with the Observant Franciscan monastery in Donegal which had been founded by his family in the last decades of the fifteenth century. Earlier in that century the Observant Movement had begun in an Augustinian monastery in the west of Ireland and soon spread throughout the other Orders. As the name suggests, its aim was to reform the friaries by encouraging the friars to follow a closer observance of the rule of their founder. In 1588 the Donegal friary was plundered by the English who established a garrison there but they were driven out by Red Hugh after his escape from Dublin Castle. He often stayed in the monastery and held important meetings there with Spanish emissaries. Before the battle of the Curlews on 15 August 1599, according to the Four Masters, O'Donnell 'observed the fast in honour of the Blessed Virgin as was his wont and Mass was celebrated for him and his army in general. He received communion after making his confession and doing rigid

Friars blessing
Irish chieftains.
Derricke

penance for his sins, and he ordered his forces to pray fervently for the
health of their souls and to save them from the English.'

The Franciscan Florence Conry became the confessor and mentor of
Red Hugh and was later to accompany him to Spain after the defeat at
Kinsale. Conry was the founder of St Anthony's College in Louvain in
1606 and later was named Archbishop of Tuam. He was born near the
village of Elphin in County Roscommon and belonged to one of the

most highly prestigious literary families in Ireland. He studied in Salamanca before joining the Franciscans and later went on to play an important role in Irish affairs at the Spanish court. Franciscan friars, like Conroy, spearheaded the Counter-Reformation in Ireland and played a vital role in preserving the old religion.

Florence Conry.
Mural,
St Isidore's,
Rome

Chapter Four

'Spanish Ale'

THE SPANISH FORCE, about 4,000 strong, under the command of Juan del Áquila, put in at Kinsale on 21 September 1601. The fleet consisted of about twenty-five sailing ships, of which seventeen were men-of-war, six galleons and the rest small boats of a hundred to a hundred-and-fifty tons. Rumours had been rife all that year of the imminent arrival of the Spaniards and the English were just as well aware of that probability as were the Irish. As early as Easter there was 'a general expectation of the Spanish before St James tide and that they make no doubt of their coming.' In July two Spanish ships landed in Killala with money and munitions and the Spaniards assured O'Donnell 'that they should presently have aid'. But as the summer turned into autumn the threat had receded. In early September, Mountjoy himself was 'rather of opinion since they have waited so long they will not come this winter'. Luckily for him he was in Kilkenny when the news arrived and, gathering all the men he could lay his hands on, he made hot-foot for the south.

O'Neill's disappointment at the choice of Kinsale, the furthest point away from his power-base in Ulster, can only be guessed at. He had expected them to land at Donegal or Killybegs but would have been happy if they came in at Killala or Sligo. Not only was Kinsale the wrong place, but it was also the wrong time of the year, and the wronged-sized force. He had always requested a minimum of 6,000 men if they were planning a Munster landing. Had they landed in Ulster or Connacht, 3,000 might well have sufficed with the numbers O'Neill and O'Donnell could then muster. His own choice of a landing place would have been Drogheda, but the Spaniards wisely rejected anywhere on the east coast as there they would have to run the gauntlet of an encounter with the English navy.

O'Neill and O'Donnell were now in a quandary, unsure what to do. At first they sent word to del Áquila to re-embark and make for Sligo but the Spaniards were unwilling to undertake what could be a perilous voyage round the west coast. The Earls had no option but to head for Kinsale. O'Donnell had collected all his forces at his castle in Ballymote and in the first week of November began to march southwards through County Roscommon, east Galway to the Shannon and then on to Kinsale. By then the Spaniards were shut into Kinsale and preparations were being made for the reduction of the town. O'Neill followed and later described the journey: 'In mid-winter they had to march a distance of about one hundred leagues through enemy territory, passing many rivers and forced to make bridges.' It was an heroic march and by the time they reached Kinsale, they had a combined force of about five-and-a-half thousand and took up their position surrounding the English, who in turn were surrounding the Spanish in Kinsale.

Mountjoy, despite his position wedged in between the two opposition forces, was eager to fight. Contrary to all their previous engagements, it was the Irish who were the first to commit themselves. They moved forward early on Christmas Eve but, finding the English on the alert, they withdrew again. Mountjoy decided to gamble and, with his superior cavalry strength, decided to charge Tyrone's infantry, which quickly broke. The battle was over in a little over a half an hour and the Irish were scattered with heavy losses. The Spanish took no part in the battle as the Irish failed to reach the pre-appointed meeting place.

Immediately after his defeat at Kinsale, O'Neill began to march swiftly northwards. There were complaints afterwards that the English forces did nothing to impede his progress. It was suggested that O'Neill sent runners ahead to spread the rumour that he had won the battle of Kinsale which would explain the reluctance of his enemies to tangle with

Two days after the battle of Kinsale, and while O'Neill was making his way northwards, Red Hugh set out for Spain to seek further help. He had already designated his brother Rory to succeed him as chieftain of the O'Donnells. He sailed from Castlehaven in the ship of a Spanish general who was reporting back to Philip III on the outcome, while del Águila and his force remained in Kinsale awaiting instructions. He was accompanied by the Franciscan, Florence Conry, who had come to Kinsale with the Spanish force. The O'Donnell poet wrote:

Rob soraidh t'eachtra, a Aodh Ruaidh
an Coimsidh do-chí ár n-anbhuain,
gabhadh Sé th'innfheitheamh Air,
go mbé ag rinnfheitheamh romhaibh.
Auspicious be your journey, Red Hugh!
The Lord God who sees our distress,
He takes upon him your care,
May He prepare your path before you.

After a stormy passage lasting seven days they made land at Luarca on the coast of Asturias. The King was then on tour and O'Donnell made his way to La Coruña to await his return. He was summoned to meet the King at about four hundred kilometres from La Coruña and he made his way there, accompanied by some Irish gentlemen as well as Florence Conry. There he made his plea for further help which was favourably received. At Zamora he also met his nephew, fifteen-year-old Henry O'Neill, then a student at the university of Salamanca. He was the son of Hugh O'Neill and Siobhán O'Donnell, Red Hugh's sister, and had been sent by his father in 1600 to be educated in Spain.

While Red Hugh was returning to La Coruña, news reached the court of del Águila's surrender at Kinsale. Fearful that the king might change his mind, Red Hugh sought another audience and this was granted. The king was now at the royal castle of Simancas, a short distance south of Vallodolid. There Red Hugh fell ill and just a little over a fortnight later he died.

Mac an Bhaird seemed to have a premonition about his death:

Na laoich, a llos a n-annsa,
na mná, na meic eagalsa,
clanna ar saor, meic ar moghadh,
dheit, a Aodh, fá énomhan.
Your warriors, by reason of their love,
Women, clerics,
The children of the nobles, the sons of our serfs,
They are all uneasy about you, Hugh.

It was rumoured that he was poisoned, a widely accepted method of political assassination at the time. Several such attempts had been made to dispose of O'Neill, one allegedly using a sacred host. 'This was a just, good and laudable plan,' according to a contemporary, 'to secure the slaying of so great a rebel who had jeopardised her Majesty's States.' O'Donnell's poisoner was named as James Blake from Galway who was then in Vallodolid. Prior to sailing from Cork to Spain, Blake had an interview with George Carew, the President of Munster, who later wrote that Blake 'is gone into Spayne with a determination ... to kyll O'Donnell', to which he added 'God give him strength and perseverance.' There is little doubt that Blake was a spy and Red Hugh himself had warned the Spanish authorities to have no truck with him. But there is strong evidence that O'Donnell died from natural causes. Florence Conry, who was with him all throughout his illness and death, never mentions the possibility of poisoning. Blake was arrested shortly afterwards and closely questioned in Valladolid prison, but there was no mention of him having anything to do with O'Donnell's death.

The body of Red Hugh, clothed in a Franciscan habit, was brought from Simancas to Valladolid in a four-wheeled hearse accompanied by a great number of dignitaries and surrounded by royal guards with blazing torches, for burial in the monastery of St Francis there. That haunting melody with its evocative lyrics, *Róisín Dubh*, is thought to have been composed as a lament for Red Hugh.

A Róisín ná bíodh brón ort ...
Tá na bráithre ar teacht thar sáile,
Is ag triall an muir ...
My darling little Rose, let be there no sorrow about what happened to you,
A blessing is coming for you from the Pope in Rome,
The friars are coming over the sea and ploughing the waves,
And Spanish wine will not be spared on my little dark Rose.

Friars, like Florence Conry and a multitude of others, were returning to Ireland and played a huge part in fomenting the Catholic resistence movement there. The wine then in Ireland was largely from Spain, and was referred to as *Iníon Rí na Spáinne*, the King of Spain's daughter, here a metaphor for Spanish military help.

James Clarence Mangan penned his own lines on Red Hugh's death:
'O think of Donnell of the ships, the Chief whom nothing daunted -
See how he fell in distant Spain, unchronicled, unchaunted!'

Red Hugh's memory was later wrapped in an aura of heroism and saintliness and he quickly became an icon of Gaelic Catholic nationalism, with the help of the *Annals of the Four Masters*, Lughaidh O'Clery's *Beatha Aodha Ruaidh Uí Dhomhnaill*, and that greatest nationalist myth-maker of all, the Ulster Protestant John Mitchel, who penned *The Life and Times of Hugh O'Neill* in 1845, aptly described by O'Faolain as 'a slight and unreliable book'.

a returning victorious army. Meanwhile, once back in Ulster, O'Neill evaded his enemies while making peace overtures to Mountjoy. At the same time, he sent a message to Philip III and Archduke Albert saying that if Spanish help did not arrive before May 1603, a ship should be sent to carry him and his followers away 'from the fury of their enemies'.

Treaty of Mellifont 1603

In February that year, Elizabeth instructed Mountjoy to assure O'Neill 'of his life, liberty and pardon upon some conditions'. The following month O'Neill signed the Treaty of Mellifont, unaware that

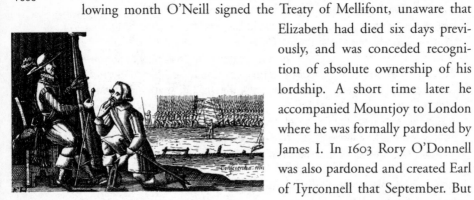

O'Neill's submission to Mountjoy

Elizabeth had died six days previously, and was conceded recognition of absolute ownership of his lordship. A short time later he accompanied Mountjoy to London where he was formally pardoned by James I. In 1603 Rory O'Donnell was also pardoned and created Earl of Tyrconnell that September. But the Treaty of Mellifont soon proved to be a brittle settlement for the northern Earls. The English authorities continued over the next few years to whittle away at their prerogatives, creating a nine-county province with sheriffs, justices of the peace and other officials. It is somewhat ironic that Elizabeth shired the country, dividing it into counties, which the Gaelic Athletic Association would later, through their All-Ireland football competition, make the most popular of all regional divisions.

The English maintained a strong military presence with garrisons in a network of strongholds. Gradually they established central control and introduced stabilised landholding, by insisting judicially that all Irish land must descend according to the common law. The best that O'Neill could hope for was to end his days on an ever-dwindling power base and reduced fortunes. The news of Maguire's arrival in Lough Swilly put him in an intolerable position. If Tyrconnell and Maguire departed without him, the probability was that he would not be allowed return from England where he had been summoned. He had no option but to join them.

Chapter Five

'A Stormy Passage'

MAC AN BHAIRD records the Flight in verse:

Anocht is uaigneach Éire
do bheir fógra a fir-fhréimhe
gruaidhe a fear 'sa fíonnbhan fliuch,
treabh is iongnadh go huaigneach.

Lonely Ireland tonight,
The banishment of her true race
Has moistened the cheeks of her men and fair women,
Wondrous for her tribe to be lonely.

They set sail at midnight on Friday, 14 September, with a steady south-westerly wind. They clung to the Donegal coast, passing Sligo Bay until they came within sight of Croagh Patrick. Fearing an encounter with some of the English fleet out of Galway, they pushed out to sea, heading for Spain as directly as they could. On Sunday, 15 September, they ran into stiff headwinds, making it impossible to continue towards Spain. Provisions were also running scarce and they decided to head towards France, which was then about two days away. Around midnight on Tuesday the wind strengthened and the waves rose suddenly and violently and the storm lasted for thirteen days. 'Only thanks to the Trinity who,' according to Ó Cianáin, 'saved the ship and its occupants from drowning.' The Earls decided, because of the scarcity of their food and drink and above all 'because of all the hardship and sea

41

sickness they had received up to that', to make straight ahead towards France. In the misty morning light they could make out the islands of Jersey and Guernsey, then in English hands. That night they were boarded by a pilot and the following morning he steered them into Quillebeuf on the south side of Le Havre. They landed there at midday on Thursday, 4 October, the feast of St Francis, and the twenty-first day since they had set out. By then, all they had left to drink was five gallons of beer and less than one barrel of water. Had they sailed directly from Rathmullan to Quillebeuf, the voyage was about 800 miles.

They hired boats and sent the women and children up the river Seine to Rouen. The following day, as the main party were about to leave, they were arrested by the governor of Quillebeuf who sent them to the governor of Normandy, the Duke of Montpensier and he detained them while he reported their arrival to the King of France and awaited his instructions. Matthew Tully was sent post-haste to Paris where the King, on his return from hunting, gave him an audience. The King's secretary assured him that they would receive a friendly answer from the King.

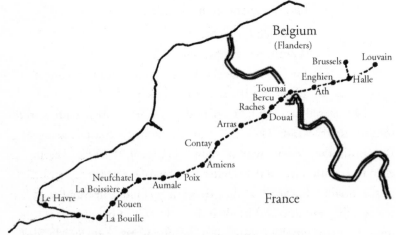

Le Havre to
Louvain
4 October –
9 November

Ever since news of their Flight had reached the English court, a massive diplomatic campaign was launched across Europe to discredit the fugitives who were described by King James as 'silly worms of the earth,' though he added the proviso, 'unless they be assisted by any foreign power'. The English ambassador, Sir George Carew, also sought an audience with the King, who chose to go hunting for three days before granting him one. And then he informed the ambassador 'that France was a free country for passengers' and that after Montpensier had given them his word, the King could not revoke it.

The Irish had to cross France to reach Flanders, the nearest Spanish territory. Again Tully was sent on ahead to alert O'Neill's son, Henry, by now colonel of the Irish in Flanders, that they were on their way and to meet them at the border. The women waited anxiously for a week in Rouen after they were informed that the main party had been arrested. On Saturday they were approached by the governor of Rouen who ordered them to leave the city without delay or else return to their ship. There was great relief on Sunday evening when the Earls and their party rode into Rouen with a passport from the King of France. They spent a day in Rouen, capital of Normandy where, with thirty-three parish churches and fourteen monasteries, Ó Cianáin was greatly impressed by 'cumhacht na hEaglaise naofa', (the power of the holy church).

Henry IV of France, originally Henry de Navarre and a Protestant, who after the War of the Three Henrys acquired the throne of France and promptly converted to Catholicism, remarking cynically that 'Paris vaut bien une messe' (Paris is well worth a Mass), and insuring that France would continue as 'la fille la plus aineé de l'église', (the eldest daughter of the church), a title she held since the end of the fifth century when the Frankish king, Clovis, was baptised. Henry was the first of the Bourbons to occupy the French throne, which was to remain in the family down to the French Revolution and beyond. With typical Gallic arrogance, Henry regarded himself as the greatest soldier of his age, the Spanish soldier Conde de Fuentes as second, and O'Neill as third.

On 15 October, they left Rouen with thirty-one on horseback, two coaches, three wagons and about forty on foot, and they covered the thirty kilometres to La Boissière. The following day they travelled fifty-eight kilometres through Neufchatel and Aumale to Poix. From there they passed through Amiens, capital of Picardy, only stopping to visit the thirteenth-century cathedral where they saw the 'head of John the Baptist'. There were a number of other churches then in western Europe with shrines claiming to house that saint's head.

Chapter Six

Spanish Flanders

THEY SPENT THE NIGHT AT CONTAY, becoming anxious as they approached the border between France and Flanders, and they mounted an armed guard there all night. From Contay they crossed the border into Spanish Flanders and reached Arras where they were met by Eoghan McMahon, who had come from Douai, having recently been named Bishop of Clogher (he was later to become Archbishop of Dublin) and who accompanied them back to Douai. Here they were greeted by Christopher Cusack, a Meath priest of Old-English background who founded the Irish college there in 1594, another in Antwerp in 1600, and later, others in Brussels, Lille and Tournai, which catered mostly for Old-English townsmen. The college in Douai illustrates how the religious conflict in Ireland was beginning to blunt the racial differences between the Old-English and the Irish, as an English spy reported to London in 1600: '... Tyrone, by name, is daily prayed for there: they all speak Irish and it is to be feared that those young gentlemen, the offspring of the colonies of the English conquest, may become in language and disposition fermented with the ancient hatred of Irish to English.' The rules of the Irish college in Tournai only permitted the students to speak in Latin or Irish.

O'Neill had already written two letters from Ireland in 1599, one to Philip III and the other to the Archduke Albert, seeking help for 'our college at Douai, containing nearly one hundred students'. In 1604 it was receiving an annual grant from Spain of 500 florins. In fact, the very last letter from O'Neill and O'Donnell before they left Flanders in February 1608 was a plea to Philip III to continue to help the college, which 'is afflicted with much poverty and want'.

In the college they were also met by the two Franciscans, Florence Conry and Robert Chamberlain and O'Neill was honoured by a Latin oration where the battle of the Yellow Ford was evoked, claiming that O'Neill and his allies had killed 50,000 enemies and captured another 3,000. They were also received in the English college in Douai where they were presented with an address in English. Later the Irish party visited the Irish College in Antwerp which Ó Cianáin described as 'very beautiful, with numerous apartments and many students'. There was a Spaniard in charge of the college who insisted on providing them with a banquet. This was probably not the Irish college but another one, where the Irish students studied. Irish colleges were then hostels which housed a number of students and the one in Antwerp was described in 1522 as 'a house supported by offerings for Masses and the charity of the people', with about a dozen students.

By now the Irish Continental Colleges movement was well under way. Not surprisingly, the earliest colleges were established in Spain or in the Spanish Netherlands, where Florence Conry established in Louvain, just before the Earls left Ireland, a college for Irish Franciscan friars in a house at the back of St Anthony's church. Later the colleges movement spread to France where a college was set up in Bordeaux in 1603. Many of these colleges were placed under the control of the Jesuits who, after the Council of Trent, made the education of priests one of their major priorities. An Irish college had been founded in Lisbon by an Irish Jesuit, John Howling, in 1590 – a year before Trinity College in Dublin which was reserved exclusively for Protestants – another in Salamanca by a Clonmel Jesuit, Thomas White, in 1592 and a third in Santiago de Compostella in the early years of the next century. Individual students had been frequenting European universities for years, such as Florence Conry and Maurice Dunleavy in Salamanca and, where they formed a group, as in Paris, an enterprising priest like John Lee brought them together to form an Irish community in one of the university colleges there, but this new intiative was designed to provide education for the

Irish Continental Colleges

Irish priesthood as a whole. The existence of these colleges was widely known in Ireland and there were some priests and students who boarded the ship at Rathmullan with the Earls for the express purpose of going to Flanders to study. Later, Matthew Tully presented a memorial to Philip III of Spain with a list of five priests, Dermot and Patrick Loughran, Neill Mac Tiernan, Turlough Slevin and Brian Gormley, as well as six students, Patrick Mac Henry and Patrick MacCormack O'Hagan, Edmund Ó Maolchraoibhe, Fergus Campbell, Matthew Traynor and Walter Rath, from O'Neill's entourage, who studied in the Irish College in Douai, and the others remained in Flanders to study. One other priest, Dermot O Doolin, remained to study in the Irish College in Douai, and five students, Brian Ó Muiríosa, Niall MacDavitt, Connor Óg Devanney, Denis Coghlan and Brian Hegerty, from Tyrconnell's party, also remained to study in Flanders.

The returning priests were already making a huge impact on the Counter-Reformation in Ireland, as London was only too well aware. It was reported that: 'The whole country does swarm with Jesuits, seminaries, massing-priests, yea and friars and these do keep such continual and daily buzzing in the poor people's ears that they are not only led from all duty and obedience to their prince but also drawn from God by superstitious idolatry and so brought headlong by heaps into hell.'

These were the shock troops in Ireland, and their return there from Europe was causing paranoia among English officials, one of whom informed Sir Robert Cecil in 1601:

'There is a number of seminary priests in this country who by their wicked and pestilent persuasions stir all those that be evil affected and disposed to rebellion and to seduce the ignorant sort of people from coming to hear divine service. This pestilent sept, if there were order taken for their banishment, and fines and exactions laid upon those that would give them entertainment and keep them in their houses, there would not be such treason and great abuses daily committed in this kingdom.'

By 1604 there were 'swarms of titulary bishops, seminaries, Jesuits, priests and friars' in the country and the government believed that 'except they be banished the land, and their relievers punished, it will be over hard to plant a learned ministry, the people are so carried away with the enticements of this rabble ...' In March 1606 Sir Arthur Chichester informed the Earl of Salisbury: 'The priests, Jesuits and seminaries within this land ... fullfreighted with malice, are busying in plotting and continuing innovation, in order to withdraw the hearts and obedience of the people', and his advice regarding priests whom he calls 'catterpillars' was to 'hang them by martial law and to confiscate the goods, or to imprison the bodies of such as are known to harbour or relieve them.'

The following year, the government admitted that there were 'more priests here than His Majesty has soldiers ...: They have so gained the women that they are in a manner all of them absolute recusants ... The people in many places resort to mass now in greater multitudes, both in town and country, than for many years past.' The trend continued with 'continual flocking of such locusts into the realm' and warrants should be issued 'to castigate them like rogues and beggars by martial law'. Finally, in May 1614 a 'Proclamation against the Toleration of Popery' was issued commanding that 'all titulary archbishops, bishops, deans, vicars-general, Jesuits, friars, seminary priests and other priests depart the realm of Ireland before 30 September next.'

The English ambassador in Brussels singled out what he called the 'perfidious Machiavellian friars at Lovayne' as especially dangerous, as they 'seek by all means to reconcile their country men in their affections, and to combine those who are descended from the English race and those who are mere Irish in a league of friendship in concurrence against your Majesty and the true religion. This is done by the advice and approbation of Spain for the backing of Tyrone and the weakening of your Majesty's party in Ireland.'

The Irish colleges movement originated from two separate events – the setting up of seminaries for the training of priests following the Council of Trent, and the prohibition of Catholic education in Ireland by the English government. Following the formula adopted at the Diet of Augsburg, *cujus regio, ejus religio,* (the religion of the ruler will be the religion of the people), Ireland became almost the only country in Christendom who did not follow the religion of their ruler. 'Perversely, most of the King's Irish subjects gave their allegiance to a church which was not the church of their civil ruler.' It was to put them on a collision course with the government in Ireland which was to last for at least two centuries.

Irish Street, Rome, site of the original Irish College

San Clemente,
Rome

St Isidore's,
Rome

The Irish Continental Colleges continued to expand in the seventeenth and early part of the eighteenth centuries, with colleges founded at Rouen, Charleville, Toulouse, Poitiers and Nantes in France, at Seville, Madrid, and Alcalá in Spain. In some places several Irish colleges were established, such as Louvain which had three, Franciscan, Dominican and Pastoral, Rome with four, Franciscans, Irish College, Dominicans and Augustinians, and Lisbon with two, St Patrick's, and Dominican.

Luke Wadding, from a Waterford merchant family, was the founder of the Irish Franciscan College in Rome, St Isidore's, in 1625, almost a decade after O'Neill's death, and with the help of Cardinal Ludovisi, protector of Ireland, of the Irish College itself in via degli Ibernesi, three years later. Luke Wadding was a towering figure, on a par, if not above, Florence Conry, not only in the Irish community in Rome and in Ireland itself, but

Luke Wadding. Mural, St Isidore's, Rome

also in the inner sanctums of the Vatican. Wadding was one of Europe's leading scholars, a theologian, poet, historian, scholar and linguist as well as being a member of various Roman congregations, holy office, index etc. It was said that he had declined the offer of a red hat and that he was the only Irishman ever to receive votes in a papal conclave. He established a Scotist school of philosophy in St Isidore's based on the origin, life and works of the medieval Franciscan, John Duns Scotist, whom Wadding claimed was an Irishman. Wadding played a large part in the politics of Ireland between 1625 and 1652 and in the affairs of the Confederation of Kilkenny, and was responsible for sending Hugh O'Neill's sword to his nephew, Owen Roe O'Neill, who had earlier won the Battle of Benburb and who had assumed the leadership of the Irish after the death of Hugh's last surviving son, John. Wadding died in 1657, his last days clouded by the fact that his advice was no longer heeded on Irish affairs, and the appalling havoc wreaked by Cromwell on his native land.

By the end of the eighteenth century there were some thirty Irish colleges extending from Lisbon to Vielun in Poland and from Nantes to Prague, where the Franciscans had a college housing fifty friars. About 1780 it was estimated that the total complement of students and clerics in all the Irish colleges abroad was approximately six hundred. Of these, the most important numerically were the two colleges in Paris, Collège des Lombards, which housed about one hundred and eighty priests, and Collège des Irlandais, with about eighty students, and Nantes which had about eighty priests. Colleges such as Alcalá, Toulouse, Santiago and surprisingly, the Irish College in Rome, usually catered for about a dozen students or less, while the Franciscan colleges in Louvain, Rome and Prague averaged about fifty and the Dominican colleges in Louvain, Lisbon, and Prague about half that number.

Other important consequences followed the establishment of these colleges. Irish nationalism became identified with Catholicism. There are no words in the Irish language for Catholics or Protestants; the former were simply called *Éireannaigh*, while the latter were known as *Sasanaigh* or *Albanaigh*. They also contributed to the extraordinary position held by priests in the minds and hearts of the people, epitomised in the 'soggarth aroon' epithet. Of the two classes who emigrated to Europe, soldiers and priests, with the exception of Owen Roe O'Neill and Thomas Preston and a small number of followers, only the priests returned and, with the demise of the Gaelic chieftains, they came to be regarded as the natural leaders of their people. Because Irish colleges were nearly always established in university cities, and the Irish followed university courses there, they were polyglots, with Irish, English and Latin, and Spanish or French

Left to right:
Irish
Franciscan
College of the
Immaculate
Conception,
Prague.
Collège des
Lombards,
Paris

depending on which university they attended. The result was that Irish priests were then probably the best educated clergy in the church. Elsewhere, like in France, each diocese set up its own seminary and their students rarely attended universities.

The Irish colleges continued to flourish until the French Revolution when most of them were confiscated. In 1795 the English government, fearing that Irish priests educated in France would return to Ireland infected with revolutionary ideas, decided to open the Royal College of St Patrick at Maynooth for the education of Irish priests. Their fears could not be more unfounded. The priests and students who survived the Revolution and, particularly, the Reign of Terror, were far from enthusiasts for revolution. The Irish College in Paris was converted into a prison where, among others, the Irish students were detained while their superiors were incarcerated elsewhere. Peter Flood from Longford, who later became one of the first Presidents of Maynooth, was miraculously rescued from the September Massacres. The use of the Irish College was later restored, but though it was now surplus to requirements, it continued to provide for about a hundred students, because it was highly endowed with burses. It closed down at the outbreak of the Second World War, with only the rector and concièrge remaining on, rearing rabbits and growing vegetables to feed themselves. After the war it was occupied by a Polish seminary until recent times when it became the Irish chaplaincy in Paris together with a *Centre Culturel Irlandais*.

'Gosh! I must be losing the sight of my sound eye!'

The 'College of the Noble Irish' in Salamanca closed during the Spanish Civil War when the students were at their summer house in Santander. Their families in Ireland were worried about their safety and requested the Irish government to intervene. President De Valera asked the British government to send a destroyer to rescue the Irish students. The irony of a Spanish-named President asking the English to rescue the Irish from Spain was not lost on Charlie Kelly in *Dublin Opinion*. He depicted the one-eyed Admiral Nelson climbing down his pillar in O'Connell Street peering at the headline in a Dublin evening newspaper: 'De Valera thanks British Navy.'

Later, Bishop Michael Browne of Galway led a delegation to Spain to inform the government there that they were leaving Salamanca. They had an interview with General Franco, who tried to persuade them to stay, indicating that Spain would help financially. When his offer was rejected, Franco declared that 'If Ireland ever again needed help, Spain would be ready', suggesting a better knowledge of the history between the two countries than was then current in Ireland. For the Irish bishops, it was just another in a long series of own goals. Just a few short years later, John XXIII made an appeal for volunteer priests to work in South America, which was answered by numerous Irish priests, who had difficulty finding a place to learn Spanish. Architecturally, Salamanca was the gem in the crown of Irish Colleges, described as a masterpiece of the Spanish Renaissance, and had come into Irish hands through the good offices of the Duke of Wellington.

The Dominicans and Franciscans managed to hold on longer to their colleges. The Dominicans finally gave up Corpo Santo in Lisbon in the eighties, while the future of San Clemente in Rome seems reasonably assured due to the discovery of substantial archaeological remains underneath the building which means it will continue as a major tourist attraction and a viable commercial enterprise. The Franciscan friary of St Anthony's in Louvain was suppressed in 1797 but bought back in 1927. More recently it became a centre for Irish-European studies. St Isidore's in Rome has been ceded to the general Franciscan order while the Irish Franciscans hope to maintain a small presence there.

After spending four days in Douai, the Earls continued on to Tournai, Ath, Enghien and finally Halle, on the last day of October, when they met Henry, O'Neill's second son, by Siobhán O'Donnell. The year after he arrived in Salamanca he caused a bit of a sensation by taking the Franciscan habit. Pressure was put on him by the King, his prime minister and the nuncio to leave the order. The Salamancan theologians deemed it a mortal sin for him to continue there. Not yet twenty years old, he was made colonel of the new Irish regiment in the Spanish army which was based in Brussels. Ten of those who accompanied O'Neill on the flight elected to remain in Flanders to serve in the Irish regiment. These included four O'Neills, Cormac, Ferdinand, Hugh MacHenry and Hugh MacBrian O'Neill, a nephew of the Earl, as well as Denis Hagan, George Inginghan, George Moore, John Rath, Peter Preston and Patrick O'Quinn. Twelve of those with O'Donnell also remained to serve and these included five Gallaghers, Charles MacArt, Turlough Carragh, Charles McTomelin, Hugh Óg MacTuathail and Tuathal as well as Denis Sweeney, John MacPhilips, William Lynch, Charles Brown, Naughtan O'Donnell and Donal Óg O'Donnell.

Later in Rome, O'Neill pleaded on behalf of 1,200 of his former comrades-in-arms who were driven out of the country to fight for the King of Sweden against the King of Poland. They switched sides, preferring to fight for the Catholic Poles rather than the heretic Swedes, which did them little good as after three years' service, the Polish King dismissed them without paying them. 'Like another race of gypsies they now wander through the world lost.' Some of them had approached O'Neill and he appealed to Spain to accept them in the Irish Regiment in Flanders. Philip III wrote to the Archduke 'to examine what could be done with them.'

The Irish regiment in Flanders was the first of a long line of Irish regiments in continental armies. Regiments were also established in Spain, such as Hibernia, Ultonia, and Mahoney's. Later that century, with the defeat of James II by William of Orange at the Battle of the Boyne and the subsequent Treaty of Limerick, enormous number of James' Irish army, about 12,000, later designated the 'Wild Geese', followed him to France where they joined newly established Irish regiments there, notably,

Irish Regiments

Berwick's, Burke's, Clare's, founded by the O'Brien family, Dillon's regiment, Galmoy, founded by Butlers, as well as numerous other regiments such as Fitzjames', Lee's, Walsh's, Lally's, Mountcashel's, Nugent's, Sheldon's, Rothe's, and Hamilton's. The members of these regiments were mercenary soldiers, who sold their services, if not to the highest bidder, at least to whatever country could provide them with a modest income.

This was, perhaps, Ireland's biggest brain drain. The Jacobites as they were called in France made a considerable contribution to the host country in a wide range of areas other than the military. Richard Contillon, a banker and economist, has been called the 'father of political economy'. Richard Hennessy settled in Cognac where he established the famous brandy distillery.

Perhaps the most distinguished soldier of the Irish regiments was Patrick Sarsfield, who was struck by a musket ball and mortally wounded at the Battle of Landen in 1693 and whose alleged last words as his blood poured forth, 'Oh that this was for Ireland', fired the imagination of an early generation of schoolboys following Irish independence, as well as the couplet:

'In far foreign fields from Dunkirk to Belgrade,
Lie the soldiers and chiefs of the Irish Brigade.'

In fact, there was no Irish Brigade, just a large number of particular regiments, usually founded by colonel-proprietors who recruited soldiers largely from their own extended families and the regions of their origins in Ireland. The most notable battle, in which no less than six Irish regiments took part, was the battle of Fontenoy in 1745, later immortalised by the stirring poem of Thomas Davis. Victory was attributed to a magnificent Irish charge, during which the Irish are said to have shouted: 'Cuimhnigí ar Luimneach agus feall na Sasanach', (Remember Limerick and English treachery).

The Irish regiments in the French army were suppressed during the French Revolution but later revived by Napoleon in the form of the Irish Legion. One of its best-known recruits was Myles Byrne, a former United Irishman from Wexford whose Memoirs give an account of the campaigns of the Legion.

In the nineteenth century an Irish Brigade was formed under the leadership of Myles O'Reilly from Longford to defend the Papal States against Italian nationalists. Part of this brigade were detailed to guard the residence in Spoleto (through which the Earls passed on the Flight) of the archbishop who later succeeded Pius IX as Pope Leo XIII.

The last military adventure from Ireland took place during the Spanish Civil War when Irishmen went to Spain to fight on both sides with the Irish Brigade under General O'Duffy on Franco's side and others fighting with the International Brigade.

Irish Regiments of France. Reproduced in R. Hayes, *Irish Swordsmen in France*

In Halle the Irish Earls were visited by Marqués Ambrosio Spinola, a wealthy Italian nobleman, who was then commander-in-chief of the army in Flanders and who some days later entertained them to a sumptuous banquet in his palace in Brussels, where the Marqués placed O'Neill at the head of the table, with the nuncio on his right and the Earl of Tyrconnell on his left. 'The excellent dinner which they partook of,' according to Ó Cianáin, 'was grand and costly enough for a king.' Spinola had already played a significant part in the Flight. Matthew Tully had been sent by Tyrconnell to Spain and, in February 1606, he presented a memorial from O'Neill and O'Donnell to Philip III in Valladolid requesting financial help 'by some secret means, without causing scandal in England', and without endangering the lives of the Earls to help them escape. The Spanish Council of State recommended that three thousand ducats should be given each to O'Neill and O'Donnell and that the money should be transferred to Henry O'Neill who would arrange to send it to Ireland. The King asked Spinola, who was then not only commander-in-chief of the army, but also minister of finance in Spanish Flanders, to pay out eight thousand crowns to Henry which he did in the middle of April after they were exchanged for gold. Later that year in August, the King authorised Spinola to pay 300 crowns to Florence Conry to go to Ireland to carry out his duties as the Provincial of the Irish Franciscans. The college for Irish friars which he had started in Louvain was then 'already under way'.

They also received an invitation in Halle from the Archduke Albert and on 5 November they were entertained by him and his wife, Infanta Isabel, the daughter of Philip II, in the private apartments of their palace in Binche. Among the other guests in the palace, besides the nuncio and the Spanish ambassador, was the Archduke's major-domo, Don Rodrigo de Lasso, whom O'Neill had already met when his Armada ship had been shipwrecked off the Inishowen coast in September 1588. Forty-five of the survivors, including de Lasso, were forced by Rory O'Donnell's father, to march on foot to Dublin, where he hoped to get Red Hugh's release, and fifteen died on the way. He was later sent to London where he was part of a prisoner exchange for Englishmen held in Spain. One of the Irish party was Captain Henry Hovedon, whose soldiers had killed no less than three hundred of his compatriots on that occasion. One wonders what, if any, exchanges took place between these two regarding the awful events of twenty years before.

Such receptions were anathema to the English authorities who, when they had fled in September 1607, had forecast that O'Neill and his 'train of barbarous, men, women and children ... will be taken for a company of gypsies and be exceedingly scorned'. That September, Sir Geoffrey Fenton wrote to Salisbury:

> Yet their carrying with them wife and children cannot but pretend a wicked purpose, to solicit fresh plots to the King of Spain and the Pope, for invading this realm eftsoons, with their joint forces; and for the more affirmation of the plot, they have brought their children, to be left as pledges in the hands of such as those princes shall nominate.

Fenton thought they would approach the King of Spain and 'afterwards draw up to Rome to sound the Pope'. When the English ambassador complained to the Archduke and asked him to arrest the Earls, he was told 'that they had been suffered to pass freely through France, notwithstanding the instance made to the contrary, and that the Archduke could not be accused for granting them the like liberty within his countries'.

Fenton had also suggested 'the employment of intelligencers'. In order to keep abreast of O'Neill's plans, two spies were dispatched to the Netherlands by the English secretary of state. One of them, James Rath, soon reported back that he was 'so happy as to insinuate himself into the favour of Tyrone, by means of a friar who is of special trust about him'. He hardly required the friar's help as he was a brother of John Rath, one of those who had travelled on the ship from Lough Swilly. The other spy was Jasper Travers from Munster and there was little love between the two, with Rath commenting that 'Munstermen … are noted to be always as false as the Devil.' Travers eventually confessed to O'Neill that he and others had been sent by the English to poison the Earls 'which is the cause that Tyrone has taken a straight order that there shall be no access to his kitchen'.

But the warmth of the Irish party's reception in Flanders, however gratifying it may have been, could not belie the enormous change in the realpolitk which O'Neill would soon learn, if he was not already aware of it. And the root of the problem was precisely in the territory which he was now traversing. This would become clear to him when he finally reached Louvain, which he did in November.

War had broken out in the Netherlands when Philip set out to crush the revolt of the seven Calvinist Dutch provinces, with Spinola leading the Spanish army and Maurice of Nassau, son of William the Silent, Prince of Orange, leading the Dutch with English backing. Spain was keen to come to a settlement with the Dutch, and English co-operation would be vital. In this, O'Neill and his entourage were becoming a troublesome embarrassment. The war came to a standstill in 1609 with Philip keeping Belgium, which remained Catholic, and Holland becoming independent and Protestant. A later successor, William of Orange, ensured that that colour would become indelibly etched on the Ulster landscape.

Louvain
9 November–
28 February

When O'Neill left Louvain two weeks later for Genoa, where he hoped to embark for Spain, they received a message from the Spanish ambassador that they were to remain in Namur, while Florence Conry was to return to confer with the ambassador. Conry was told that King Philip had sent instructions that O'Neill 'should not pass into Spain, to avoid giving discontentment to his Majesty James I.' James had already issued a proclamation against the Earls, designed to turn public opinion against them, which was widely circulated among the English ambassadors. They were described as conspirators and traitors who had plotted rebellion, using priests to solicit help from foreign princes. The King hoped that his proclamation would 'disperse and discredit all such untruths as these contemptible creatures shall disgorge against us', and dispel the calumnies which those slanderous, treacherous and ungrateful men might spread against his just and moderate government. The Irish were to remain in Flanders. Understandably, Conry 'was grieved at this, though I told him in the best possible manner'. The Irish party returned to Louvain where they were to remain for the next thirteen weeks, from 29 November to the 28 February. 'He will pass the winter there,' the Venetian ambassador reported, 'as a kind of hostage for the King's attitude.' The English ambassador reported triumphantly to London: 'Tyrone has not stirred out of Louvaine since he was stayed of his journey' and later he commented that the Irish 'liberally drink sack (white wine) instead of usquebaugh, for the digesting of their melancholy'.

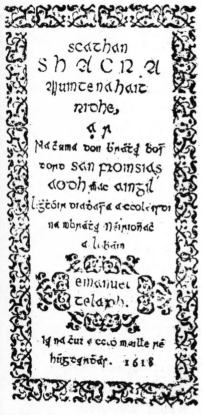

Scáthán Shacramuinte na h-aithridhe (Louvain 1618) by Aodh MacAingil

O'Neill and O'Donnell wrote an extremely long letter to Philip III – probably drafted by Florence Conry who was described as their 'interpreter and counsellor' – detailing what they called the 'eleven years war' which they waged against the English up to their defeat at Kinsale, and the persecution of Irish Catholics which was now taking place. '... it follows that Your Majesty is under the obligation of giving us the help for which we ask, not only as a Catholic King whose concern is to defend and protect all afflicted Catholics, but also … because there is no other Christian prince to defend the Catholics of Ireland against the violence which is being done to them on account of their religion …' They also mention that 'in proportion to its size, the kingdom of Ireland is one of the most abundant and well provided in Europe as regards bread, meat, fish, lard and beer.'

The Spanish Council discussed this letter in the middle of January 1608 and suggested that they should go to Rome, a suggestion first made by the Spanish ambassador in London. On the other hand, the nuncio in Brussels had already advised O'Neill to rely on the King of Spain and not on the Pope, Paul V, who did not relish having to pay the expenses of the Irish party in Rome. The nuncio tried to impress on Florence Conry that everything possible should be done to prevent O'Neill going to Rome. 'Unlike Clement VIII,' the Spanish ambassador remarked, 'His Holiness has not the soul of the prince.' The Pope's opposition was overcome by the Spanish agreeing to pay for their upkeep – 400 ducats a month to O'Neill and 300 to O'Donnell. Their presence in Flanders was now an embarrassment to the Archduke, and Spinola was asked to tell them that they should leave, which Spinola thought was 'very harsh'. The Earls were shocked at this request. 'As God is our witness,' they informed Philip III, 'we would rather have chosen to die in our country, than to see ourselves treated in this manner.'

But they had no option but to leave. Arrangements were made for the children, including O'Neill's two sons, O'Donnell's son, and the son of Caffar O'Donnell, with their nurses, tutors and servants, to remain in Louvain under the watchful eye of the friars in the college that Conry had acquired for them in 1606.

On 28 February, the Irish party, thirty-two on horseback and the ladies, Countess Catherine Magennis, Nuala O'Donnell, Rose O'Dogherty, and Bríd, O'Neill's beautiful young daughter, described as of 'marriage-able age', in a coach. It must have been heart-rending for the Countess Catherine to have to leave her two sons behind, having already left one in Ireland, and also for Rose O'Dogherty, who left her only son there.

 The college had an annual grant of 1,000 ducats from Philip III and the first novices were received there in November while the Earls were there. Ten years later the friars moved to the present college of St Anthony's after the foundation stone had been laid by Archduke Albert and Infanta Isabella.

Less than ten years later, this college was to earn the gratitude of all subsequent Gaelic scholars and historians for their extraordinary efforts in saving and copying original Irish manuscripts on the point of extinction. John Colgan established in St Anthony's a school of Irish studies where he himself compiled *Acta Sanctorum Hibernorum, The Lives of the Irish Saints*. The poet-friar, Aodh MacAingil (Hugh MacCaghwell), composed his *Scáthán Shacramuinte na hAithridhe*. Bonaventure O'Hussey's *Teagasg Críostaí* or Catechism was the first book ever printed in Irish and the font used in Antwerp was said to have been modelled on O'Hussey's own handwriting and remained the standard for Irish printing down to the middle of the twentieth century. But easily the most important enterprise undertaken by the college in Louvain was when *an bráthar bocht*, Michael O'Clery, was sent back to Ireland in 1632, where he spent five years close to the monastery in Donegal, with three others, seeking out old manuscripts from which they compiled *Anála Ríoghachta Éireann*, better known as the *Annals of the Four Masters*. O'Clery died and was buried in St Anthony's, Louvain but, ironically, the man who chronicled his country's history has no monument to mark his grave.

Anála Ríoghachta Éireann (1630-35)

News of their departure caused 'great rejoicing' in England. Among those in the Irish entourage was the spy, Rath, for whom the English had arranged payment for three or four months before the departure. The Spanish ambassador in London had warned King Philip that O'Neill's life was in danger. 'I know that they wish to kill him by poison or by any possible means, so I believe it is necessary to have him guarded.'

Chapter Seven

'A Garden in the very centre of Christendom'

Louvain to Nancy 28 February- 3 March

W HEN THE IRISH LEFT LOUVAIN everybody was convinced that their destination was Rome, that is, except the Earls themselves. Their intention was to reach Milan, a Spanish territory, where they hoped to receive a reply, this time favourable, from the King to the letter they had sent him before they set out. The English ambassador was in no doubt that O'Neill was heading to Rome 'where he can promise himself no other relief than what may be derived from bulls and benedictions', and even so he had no intention of making it any easier for them. He wrote in French to the Duke of Lorraine, whose territory the Irish were approaching, that King James expected that the 'fugitive rebels ... against whom the door to Spain was shut', would be refused entry. He also sent him a French translation of the English king's proclamation against them.

The Irish party, with an escort of the Archduke's troops, travelled from Louvain to Wavre on the first day. The next day they went to Namur where they spent the night. They left the coach there as the roads were very bad and they put the women on horseback. Colonel Henry O'Neill accompanied them as far as Namur, where they parted, father and son, never to meet again. The governor of Namur sent troops to accompany them. They then went on to Marche, to Bastogne and to Arlon. From Arlon in present-day Luxembourg, they crossed the frontier from the Netherlands into the Duchy of Lorraine. From there they passed through Longwy, Fillières and Conflans. Then they went through Mars-la-Tour, Pont-à-Mousson and finally to Nancy, the capital of Lorraine. Their journey through Lorraine to Nancy, comprising about 140 kilometres, took four days. The Irish party knew in advance that they would be given free passage through Lorraine. The English ambassador had reported in January that Maguire was absent and thought that he might have gone ahead to Rome, but he was back after a short absence and may well have gone to Lorraine to get assurances from the Duke.

The Duke of Lorraine

Charles III was then Duke of Lorraine where he had ruled for over sixty years. He wasn't even three years old when his father died and he succeeded. At sixteen he married a daughter of King Henry II of France, who was herself only eleven years old. On the evening of their arrival in Nancy, the Duke's steward arrived to invite them to the palace, but they declined, pleading tiredness after their journey. He returned the following morning with fine coaches in which they were brought to the palace where they were warmly welcomed by the Duke. At midday six of them sat down to dinner, O'Neill, O'Donnell and the Baron of Dungannon with the Duke and his two sons, who at that time were aged forty-five and thirty-seven. After dinner they were provided with two bedrooms for a siesta. Later they were accompanied back to their lodgings by the Duke's chief steward, who proclaimed under severe penalty that no one should accept gold or silver of them as long as they were in the city, but that the Duke would bear all their expenses. The Duke's sister, the Duchess of Brunswick, afterwards called on Countess Catherine at her inn. King James was so angered by the reception given them that when the Duke died a little over two months later he sent no representative to the funeral, which was commented on by the French ambassador in London.

Nancy to Milan
10-23 March

They left Nancy on Monday, 10 March, and continued through St-Nicolas, to Lunéville on the first day and thereafter, to St-Dié. Then they left Lorraine which Ó Cianáin described as 'garden in the very centre of Christendom, giving neither obedience nor submission to any king or prince in the world, but ever steadfast, strong and unbending in the faith of God's church', and crossed into Alsace which was then within the empire. They were now in the Vosges mountains and they passed through Bonhomme and Kayserberg to Colmar which Ó Cianáin mentions was under the control of 'heretics'. From there they went through Niederhergheim to Ottomarsheim and then through Bâle in Switzerland which was also occupied by heretics, and there were pictures of Luther and Calvin 'and many other wicked evil writers' in a large church in the middle of the city, which was not surprising as the famous portrait painter, Hans Holbein, lived there in the first half of the sixteenth century. He is probably best known for his portrait of Henry VIII.

They continued on to Liestal, a Catholic town. The next day they passed through Olten and Zofingen to Sursee and then to Sempach and Lucerne, surrounded by the Alps, a Catholic town where a nuncio resided. Here they put their horses into boats and rowed through the lake to Flüelen where they arrived at midnight.

Lucerne, Switzerland

Chapter Eight

The Devil's Bridge

IRONICALLY, THE NEXT DAY, St Patrick's Day, was to prove particularly eventful for the Irish party. They went to Silenen, a small town at the foot of the Saint Gotthard Pass. Ó Cianáin takes up the story: From that they advanced through the Alps. Now the mountains were laden and filled with snow and ice, and the roads and paths were narrow and rugged. They reached a high bridge called the Devil's Bridge in a very deep glen. One of O'Neill's horses, which was carrying some of his money, about one hundred and twenty pounds, fell down the face of the high, frozen, snowy cliff which was in front of the bridge. Great labour was experienced in bringing up the horse alone, but the money decided to remain, blocking the violent, deep, destructive torrent, which flows under the bridge through the middle of the glen.

O'Neill sent some people back next day to try and retrieve the money but without success. The loss of the money was a major setback. It was important not only that O'Neill reached his destination safely but that he did so in style. Europe would not be impressed by a straggling party of tattered beggars. When Dermod McCarthy and myself in 1985 first tried to find the Teufelsbrücke (the Devil's Bridge) we failed and decided to spend the night in a *pensione* in the nearest little town. Next morning while at breakfast we noticed an engraving on the wall depicting the bridge and, with directions from the *padrone*, we finally succeeded in our mission.

Devil's Bridge
(Teufelsbrücke)

They passed through the Saint Gotthard Pass to Airolo and then through a valley with a gate called the Gate of Hell, where customs had to be paid under penalty of death, and reached Faido where they spent the night. The next day they went through Bellinzona and Lugano at the head of Lake Lugano where they, with their horses, embarked on boats which took them across the lake to Capolago. The lake separated Switzerland from Italy. Ó Cianáin was very impressed by the Swiss:

It is said of the people of this country that they are the most just, honest, and untreacherous in the world, and the most faithful to their promises. They allow no robbery or murder to be done in their country without punishing it at once. Because of their perfect honour they alone are guards to the Catholic kings and princes of Christendom.

Not surprising then that the Pope should have chosen the Swiss
Guard as his personal bodyguard. The corps was instituted by Pope
Julius II (1503-13) with whom the cantons of Zurich and Lucerne
entered an agreement to supply two hundred and fifty guardsmen.
Their parade uniform was designed by Michaelangelo. Later, when
they reached Rome, the Irish saw them in action, escorting the Pope on
several occasions.

On Sunday, 23 March, they reached Milan, then a dependency of the
Spanish crown:

> The Earl of Tyrone, with his wife and about forty men of their crew,
> arrived by the way of Switzerland this last week in Milan, on horse-
> back, well armed with arquebuses and pistols, to the no small won-
> der of the beholders, the Governor there having formerly denied
> entrance into the city with arms of that quality even to the ambassa-
> dors of great princes. The Governor also sent to them immediately
> upon their arrival, his *cameriere maggiore* with banqueting stuff and
> other refreshments and with words of much affection.

Thus the English ambassador in Venice informed the King of England of their arrival in Milan. He had received this information from
the Venetian ambassador in Milan who had managed to plant a secret
agent among the Irish. The latter got his information from O'Neill's
chaplain 'who speaks Spanish admirably'. The chaplain was Robert
Chamberlain, from an Old-English family in County Louth, and it was
no surprise that he spoke Spanish fluently as he took his doctorate at
the university of Salamanca where he later taught theology. In Milan
they stayed at the 'Hosteria of the Three Kings', so-called after the sarcophagus in the nearby church of Sant' Eustorgio which once contained
the remains of the Magi who visited the Christ-child in Bethlehem. It
was said that the remains of the three kings were given to Archbishop
Eustorgio by the Emperor Constantine but were later taken by Freder-
ick Barbarossa to the cathedral in Cologne. Nevertheless, according to
Ó Cianáin, the sarcophagus was exhibited to the public on each feast of
the Epiphany, as well as a piece of the gold which was part of the gifts
they offered to the Holy Family.

The Governor of Milan, the Conde de Fuentes, had already received instructions from Philip III to keep them in Milan while he found out their intentions. As early as 1602 the Conde de Fuentes had recommended that the state of Ireland be discussed by the Spanish Council of State where the King's confessor thought it would be of great importance to send help to 'the Catholics of Ireland, who, at the risk of their lives, are demonstrating every day the zeal and devotion they have for the Catholic faith and for the service of Your Majesty'. Now in March 1608, a note added to the King's letter, by the Spanish Council of State, instructed the Conde 'to treat them with particular care and to send them on their way to Rome, and if they are in need, he should provide them with whatever may appear necessary'.

Conde de Fuentes, Governor of Milan

The Conde informed King Philip of the arrival of the Earls 'and in accordance with Your Majesty's orders, I feasted them and treated them with care in as discreet and secret a manner as possible, in order both to assure them of the generosity and compassion of Your Majesty and to make them amenable to Your Majesty's wishes.' He went on to describe their state when they arrived:

> I felt the greatest pity for them; one of them brings a sister of marriageable age, and another, a wife and son; they bring also many persons who would not be parted from them. They arrived in great distress from the hardship of the journey and in such need that it was necessary to pay their hostelries.

O'Neill was determined to remain in Milan until he got a definite reply from King Philip, as he informed the Archbishop of Armagh, Peter Lombard, who was then in Rome: 'As regards our going to Rome ... we do not intend to undertake that journey without first receiving orders from the Catholic King so that he might not have an excuse to abandon us and to leave us to the sole patronage of the Pope.' The English ambassador in Venice was very much *au courant* with O'Neill's intentions, as he reported to King James: 'and there it seems, they determine to rest until answer has been had from Spain about them and accordingly to take their journey to Rome or otherwise.' Apparently, Irish émigres in Europe were buzzing with rumours of O'Neill's imminent return to Ireland with Spanish help. An English spy in Spain reported to London that he had met an Irish merchant in the port of Bayona and when he asked him about Tyrone, 'the Irishman made no answer but put his finger to his mouth and bit his nail; and in the end told him that before it were long there would be something done which men little dreamed of'. The English ambassador reported early in September: 'Ireland is quiet. There had been a rising of some scamps who expected help from other scamps, who like gypsies came over to Italy for that purpose. They failed …'

Milan
23 March –
12 April

Meanwhile, the Irish had much to see in the city of Milan, where they spent three full weeks. According to Ó Cianáin, there were no less than two hundred and forty-three churches in the city, not counting the private chapels erected by noblemen, as well as altars erected in every marketplace where Masses were celebrated every day. The *pièce de resistance* was the Duomo, the cathedral, with its large collection of relics, many of them exotic, such as the bodies of eleven of the Holy Innocents slain by Herod. It also housed the body of Charles Borromeo who had been recently Archbishop of Milan and whom everybody thought would soon be canonised. In fact, he was canonised about two and a half years later. The Irish were in Milan during Holy Week and they visited the cathedral on the evening of Good Friday when they witnessed an extraordinary sight:

> They saw many hundreds of men in a splendid procession, with lighted waxen torches about them, and their faces covered so that they might not be recognised. They were scourging, smiting and whipping their bodies until the streets and the churches in which they walked were red with blood and gore. To behold them moved one much to charity and self-examination.

Meanwhile, there was frantic diplomatic activity behind the scenes. Philip III had already written to his ambassador in Rome instructing him to speak to the Pope suggesting 'how fitting and proper it would be that His Holiness protect and help these people for, in defence of our holy religion they have lost their country and all they possessed'. He was also to spread the rumour that the Pope had sent for them 'so that no one may know or suspect that the Earls have gone to Rome on my order'. The ambassador reported that the Pope had replied that 'he would honour and favour them as much as he could' but thought he would give them nothing or very little because 'the apostolic treasury is very low and His Holiness is not very liberal'. The Pope was not prepared to state that he had sent for them but that they were coming of their own accord to seek refuge with him. From London the Spanish ambassador wrote:

> Such is the fear they have of the Earl of Tiron that they have now sent a messenger to Ireland with orders from the Viceroy not to press the Catholics, search their houses, nor punish them for hearing Mass in their homes.

This may have been in response to the English ambassador in Venice who commented on 'the Irish gypsies who are wandering from state to state and from city to city seeking support and favour under the pretext of being persecuted for the faith and for conscience, the cloak of every scamp nowadays.'

The Earls themselves were not lagging in making their own case to the Spanish King. They drafted no less than three lengthy memorials which were transmitted to Spain with a covering letter by the Conde de Fuentes. In one of them, they cite a recent Spanish authority who claimed that the Irish were descended from Milesius, a Spanish King. They had already, before leaving Flanders, sent Matthew Tully ahead to Madrid to represent them at the Spanish court and he presented a memorial to Philip III at the end of April requesting him to send an answer to the Earls. The English ambassador in Spain quickly learned of Tully, 'so notoriously known to be a solicitor for Tyrone', and his mission and made a formal complaint. But he was fobbed off by the Spanish Secretary of State who claimed that Tully 'neither brought letter in his pocket nor word in his mouth' from the Earls. The ambassador was not that easily duped. 'By God's grace,' he assured London, 'I will keep a vigilant eye upon the ways which that man will tread in.'

Chapter Nine

'All Roads lead to Rome'

THE EFFORTS OF THE EARLS and Tully were all in vain. The King was not for turning and he had already instructed the Conde de Fuentes to inform the Earls of his decision. The Earls were greatly disappointed when the Conde informed them that the King wished them to go to Rome: 'I told them that it would be of greater advantage to them to await in Rome Your Majesty's decision concerning them and this could be hastened if they begged the Pope to write to Your Majesty.' They left the King in no doubt about their disappointment:

> Although it is very much against our will that we are going there, when we remember how we served Your Majesty and what we have lost by taking up arms in your royal service and in that of the Catholic Church, we are convinced that Your Majesty is not causing us to leave your dominions in order to abandon us, but on the contrary so as to be in a position to help us with greater facility and secrecy, as the Conde de Fuentes has indicated to us.

It only remained, before they left Milan, for the Earls to negotiate with the Conde what money they would require to cover their ordinary expenses in Rome and they had no intention of selling themselves short, as the Spanish ambassador in Rome was soon to learn, much to his chagrin. 'I found them very difficult,' the Conde informed the King, 'for they say that two thousand five hundred ducats a month would not be enough for them.' He recommended that they should be given a little more than half that amount.

The English ambassador in Venice complained formally to Spain about the reception accorded to them by de Fuentes. He was kept informed by the Venetian ambassador in Milan. Early in April he reported:

> The Earl of Tyrone has been to audience of the most illustrious the Governor. They sent to fetch him at night in one of the Governor's carriages, and Don Francesco, Grand Chamberlain, and many torches. His Excellency received him even as far out as two chambers, and treated him as a grandee, accompanying him as far as the stair ... The Earl was a long hour in audience, very secret; we cannot penetrate the subject of the discussion. Every day Fuentes sends the Earl one of his carriages and his lacqueys.

A week later Tyrone, along with his wife and son, again visited the Conde where 'he was as well received as on the former occasion'. Nevertheless, the Conde put it about 'that he takes little account of Tyrone and will not supply him with money'. This was also the line taken by the Spanish authorities in Madrid who replied 'that the King of Spain had nothing to do with the matter and, in view of his well-known niggardliness, Fuentes would never give Tyrone any thing out of his own pocket'. Furthermore, they insisted 'that the Conde de Fuentes was not a man disposed to such largesse as to entertain strangers in a costly manner at his own expense'.

The English ambassador in Venice would have none of this, claiming 'that he now had reason to take this to be an affront to himself that he should think him so weakly intellegenced'. And he was right, as Ó Cianáin recorded: 'The Lords took their leave of the Count de Fuentes on the twelfth of April. He had been kindly and friendly to them at their coming, and he was sad when they left. He gave them as a token of remembrance a collection of rapiers and fine daggers, with hilts of ornamented precious stones, all gilt, and belts and expensive hangers.'

In all, the Irish party spent three weeks in Milan and, some time before they left on 12 April 1608, O'Neill was approached by an English priest on behalf of the Venetian ambassador. The Republic of Venice then enjoyed close ties with England and the Doge had no wish to upset King James. A contemporary book, thought to be the 'work of a Jesuit or some such bad character', described the Republic of Venice as 'a corpse and the King of England as a crow that settled on it'. The Venetian ambassador asked the English priest 'to inform the Earl that in view of the perfect amity which existed between the Republic and the King

Milan to Rome
12 April –
29 April 1608

ITALY

Milan
Lodi
Piacenza
Parma
Modena
Bologna
Faenza
Forligrande
Savignano
Rimini
Cattolica
Pesaro
Fano
Senigallia
Ancona
Loreto
Recanati
Macerata
Tolentino
Valcemara
Assisi
Muccia
Foligno
Nuovacasa
Verchianno
Strettura
Terni
Narni
Otricoli
Borghetto
Civita Castellana
Rignano
Castelnuovo
Rome

of England, it was Your Serenity's desire that the Earl should neither enter nor pass through your dominions.' Before ever they left Louvain, the English ambassador had already pressed the Venetian authorities to seize O'Neill if he entered their territory, though the Venetian Senate took a more compromising position, that should the Earl enter their state pressure would be put on him to leave again. The Earl was grateful for the priest's warning and promised not to take that road.

The Irish spent their first night at Lodi and the next at Piacenza, and the road between them had already been travelled by another party of Ulstermen a thousand years before. Saint Columbanus led the Irish monks on foot across the Alps. Half-way between Lodi and Piacenza is a town called San Columbano al Lambro, and about forty kilometres south-west of Piacenza Columbanus founded his last monastery at Bobbio in 613, and he died there two years later.

In Piacenza the River Po separates Lombardy from Parma which was their next destination. The Duchy of Parma was created by Pope Paul III in 1545 for his own son, Pierluigi Farnese. His descendant, Duke Rannucio, sent coaches to conduct them to his residence where 'he received them with honour and respect'. In Parma they were shown a leopard and two lions as well as two camels – 'the sight of them was very strange'. Next day they left the Duchy of Parma and crossed into Modena. Italy was then a patchwork of petty principalities and did not become a nation state until the nineteenth century, long after the emergence of strong national governments in Spain, France, England and several other countries. The delay in the unification of Italy was largely due to the existence of the Papal States which split the Italian peninsula in two and which the Irish party was now approaching.

In Bologna they were invited by the cardinal to come to supper with him but they declined, pleading fatigue. However, O'Neill called on him the next day at his large palace in the centre of the city, where he was received 'with great honour, respect and welcome'. The next day they passed through Faenza and Forligrande and Savignano where they literally crossed the Rubicon to Cesena where they rested, and then on to Rimini on the Adriatic sea and eventually they reached Cattolica.

After hearing Mass on Sunday in Cattolica, they went on through Pesaro and then Fano and Senigallia on the Adriatic coast. These

formed part of the Duchy of Urbino which was absorbed into the Papal States less than twenty years later. Senigallia was the birthplace of Pius IX (Pio Nono), whose attempts to block the unification of Italy earned him the hatred of Italian nationalists. Italian troops entered Rome at the end of September 1870 and a plebiscite the following month established the union of Rome and Italy. Pius IX became the self-styled 'prisoner of the Vatican' and it has been suggested by some that, with the loss of his temporal power, he defined the doctrine of Papal Infallibility at the first Vatican Council to enhance his spiritual authority.

Pio Nono

From there the Irish party went through Ancona to Loreto. The English Secretary of State was kept informed of the Earl's travels by a secret agent who had infiltrated the Irish party. His last news of Tyrone is from Rimini, on his way to Loreto: 'Before him was sent the Earl of Tyrconnell … with three coaches full of attendants to take up the Hosteries for the Prince; so they style Tyrone himself.'

As a leader of the Catholic struggle in Ireland on his way to pay homage to the Pope, pilgrimages to places like Loreto could only enhance his image, a fact which was not lost on the English ambassador in Venice who remarked that 'a show of religion' would do him no harm. Now as they approached Rome, O'Neill was being finally groomed for his role as the great Catholic champion, and there were no better spin-doctors to act as his mentors than the two Franciscans, Florence Conry and Robert Chamberlain, both university graduates of Salamanca in the immediate aftermath of the Council of Trent. That Council, far from pandering to the antipathy of Protestants to all practices relating to relics, pilgrimages, indulgences, religious icons, etc., clarified and reinforced its doctrinal position on these matters. Trent chose to emphasise precisely what the Protestants had condemned, among them veneration of the saints.

More recently, Kenneth Clarke, the originator of the prestigious BBC series, *Civilization*, attributed his own conversion to Catholicism to that decision of the Council and the innumerable artistic masterpieces it inspired. 'The great achievements of the Catholic Church lay in harmonising, humanising, civilising the deepest human impulses of ordinary people.'

It proved to be a public relations coup which insured that the church, with the help of the numerous artists it inspired, mostly Italian, would win hands down the battle for the hearts and minds of the people. Baroque is the style of art and architecture most closely associated with the Counter-Reformation, of which a prime example is the Jesuit church, San Ignazio, in Rome, with its ceiling and walls covered with elaborate paintings and winged angels literally dripping over their frames on to the walls, and many side-chapels dedicated to particular saints and graced with sculptures of them. It was an exuberant and extravagant style most notably illustrated by Michaelangelo's painting of the Last Judgement in the Sistine Chapel and in sculpture by Bernini's marble statue of the almost trembling body of the ecstatic St Teresa, her heart pierced by the golden arrow of a cherub. Other baroque artists included Titian, Tintoretto and Caravaggio. Copies of these Italian religious paintings were widely reproduced throughout the rest of the Catholic world, not only in Europe but also in the new churches in America, the Philippines, Goa and Central and South America and was to dominate religious imagery up to comparatively recent times.

Ireland was the sole exception: due to it being an underground church for almost two centuries, it had to wait until the second half of the nineteenth century when the parish missions caused a 'devotional revolution' and flooded the countryside with 'holy pictures'. The earliest ornamentation introduced into the chapels were the Stations of the Cross.

Relics

However, the church could have done more to authenticate the relics still revered over fifty years after Trent. Those recorded by Ó Cianáin included some of the more exotic examples such as eleven of the Holy Innocents martyred by Herod on hearing of Christ's birth, the hand of St Nicholas, the head of John the Baptist, the forefinger of the left hand of St Anne, Mary's mother, a hair of the head of Mary Magdalen, not to mention the house of the Holy Family in Loreto. Ó Cianáin gives a lengthy account of the legend that the home of the Holy Family in Nazareth was carried by angels and deposited in Loreto, which he copied from an old book. As for the True Cross, ever since it was reportedly found in Jerusalem by Constantine in the fourth century, so many fragments were dispersed throughout Christendom that it was estimated that it would require several forests to provide the timber. Hugh O'Neill himself brought a relic of the True Cross with him which he had rescued from the cathedral in Armagh which had then fallen into Protestant hands. Later, the Irish would see in many of the two hundred and forty-six churches in Rome many more relics no less exotic, including the rod of Moses and Aaron, the cradle in which the infant Jesus was placed as well as his first nappy, one of the gold coins that the Magi brought as gifts to Bethlehem, the table from which Jesus ate the last supper with his apostles, the sponge with which the soldiers gave him vinegar to drink, two thorns from the crown of thorns, the nail that went through the feet of Christ, one of the thirty pieces of silver paid to Judas, the forefinger which Thomas placed in the side of Christ, one of the arrows by which St Sebastian was put to death, the head of the Samaritan woman, the heads of St Andrew, St Luke the Evangelist, St James the Younger, St Sebastian, St Thomas of Canterbury, the hand of St Stephen as well as one of the stones with which he was stoned, the hand of St Christopher, and one of Peter's teeth.

It is somewhat surprising that Ó Cianáin, a highly educated man, a trained chronicler who recorded clinically the important events of his patron's family, should betray not the slightest scepticism when recording these relics. It should be said, however, that some of them, such as the Veronica, the towel with which Jesus wiped himself on the road to Calvary and which had imprinted on it his image, has only very recently been discounted by the church, as well as the removal of St Christopher from the calendar of saints. Even in more enlightened times people in Ireland flocked in numbers to where there were reports of moving statues.

The cult of relics was strongly embedded in local tradition and people were understandably reluctant to relinquish what their ancestors had cherished for centuries. Besides, relics were good earners, both spiritually and temporally, for the churches which housed them.

It was almost a hundred years now since the Dominican John Tetzel had launched his indulgence crusade in Germany, which justifiably raised the ire of Martin Luther, contributing in no small way to the Protestant Reformation. The crude jingle that promoted the campaign –

'As soon as the money in the coffer rings,
the soul from Purgatory's fire springs'
– provided easy ammunition for Luther to attack Rome.

While Trent continued to promote indulgences, it had gone a long way towards cleaning up its act. Ó Cianáin records that the Irish began their pilgrimage to the Basilica of Santa Maria Maggiore by going to confession and receiving Holy Communion.

At St John Lateran's, where the heads of Peter and Paul were kept, pilgrims from Rome received indulgences of three thousand years, those from elsewhere in Italy six thousand years, while the Irish received no less than twelve thousand years. The Scala Santa or Holy Stairs has twenty-eight steps which it was believed that Jesus had to climb when he was brought before Pilate. Everyone who ascends the steps on their knees are granted three years remission of their sins. But there was nothing automatic about it, as Ó Cianáin points out: 'It is expected of all that they repent, pray and invoke Almighty God with compunction of heart for all their wickedness, having the love of God and their neighbour, as they ascend that holy, blessed, meritorious stair.' Elsewhere he states in relation to somebody seeking indulgences: 'It is essential for him that he possess the love of God and his neighbour, with contrition for his sins and vices,' conditions which are not easily fulfilled.

Scala Santa, Rome

There was also a good deal of almsgiving and charity associated with the cult of relics. In Milan on the patron's day the tradesmen came in procession to the cathedral where they distributed alms and there were six days of the year when alms were distributed at each of the six gates of the city. On the feast of the Epiphany every year dowrys were given to 'nine maidens' by the superiors of the church in the same city, where the gold coin presented to the Holy Family in Bethlehem was preserved. 'Much charity and good holy deeds are performed in that city, but it would be tedious to enumerate them all.'

Having completed their pilgrimage, the Irish party set out from Loreto on 23 April and passed through Recanati and Macerata to Tolentino. On the following day they went through Valcimara, Camerino and Muccia to Nuovacasa. From there they went through Verchiano to Foligno. From there the Earl of Tyrconnell, the Baron of Dungannon, Caffar O'Donnell and Maguire, with a party of gentlemen accompanying them, made a slight detour to make a pilgrimage to Assisi where St Francis, who died in 1226, was buried. There they were met by the General of the Order and a large number of friars and they were received 'with great respect and welcome'. It was understandable why the Earl of Tyrconnell would have wanted to visit Assisi, with his family's long and close association with the Franciscans in Donegal, but it is surprising that O'Neill did not accompany them but remained in Foligno to await their return.

During this time the English ambassador, under the pseudonym of Ottavio Baldi, reported to James I: 'Four days since came unto me an Italian of middle age, sober in countenance ... He was sent from a gentleman (who) had understood that in Milan were arrived certain dangerous rebels against Your Majesty, whereof there was one said to be the head and leader of the rest, whom he would find a means to send *a casa del diavolo* ... if he might be assured it would be acceptable as a piece of service to your Majesty, as it might merit your favourable letters for his repatriation.' The ambassador gave his own opinion to the dapper Italian and would-be assassin, 'that services of this kind unto princes were commonly most obligatory when they were done without their knowledge'.

From Foligno the Irish travelled on to Strettura, Terni, Narni and Otricoli. From there they went to Tevere, 'a city where boats convey people and horses across the very strong river Tiber'. Then onto Borghetto, Civita Castellana, Rignano and Castelnuovo from where they could see 'the belfries and walls of Rome'.

Assisi

Chapter Ten

'Bulls and Benediction'

THE NEXT DAY THEY TRAVELLED the short distance to Prima Porta from where they sent messengers to alert the Roman authorities of their imminent arrival in the city. It was imperative, with the eyes of the world on them, that they arrive in style in the eternal city. Peter Lombard came to meet them with fifteen coaches, most of them drawn by six horses, sent by the cardinals. Lombard, from an old English family in Waterford, had been appointed by O'Neill as his agent in Rome and was nominated Archbishop of Armagh in 1601. The Pope ordered the English Catholics in Rome to go out to meet them. O'Neill was reported as saying to one of them, 'It is better to be poor in Rome than rich in an English prison.' They entered Rome on 29

Porto del
Populo, Rome

April by the Porta del Populo and travelled through the principal streets 'in great splendour' until they reached St Peter's in the Vatican. After a brief visit, they went to the 'splendid palace' (Palazzo Salviati or Palazzo dei Penitenzieri) in the Borgo Vecchio and Santo Spirito, which the Pope had put at their disposal. The Palazzo was built between 1480 and 1490 for Cardinal Domenico Della Rovere using the best artists of the

time, including Pinturicchio, and rivalled in magnificence the most prominent Roman palaces. Subsequent occupants included Cardinal Giovanni Salviati in 1524 and later the Penitentiaries, an order of priests whose task was to confess pilgrims in St Peter's. Since 1950 the Palazzo houses Hotel

Palazzo Salviati (Hotel Columbus)

Columbus on the Via della Conciliazione which leads directly into St Peter's Square. The English ambassador reported O'Neill's arrival to London: 'Now all Italy rings for his reception in Rome.'

Since they left Ireland, they had covered almost 4,000 kilometres, 1,200 on sea, the rest on horseback. The journey took them over five and a half months, passing through 109 towns, and eight different countries – France, Spanish Flanders, Germany, the Swiss cantons, the duchies of Lorraine, Parma, Milan and the Papal States. When the Spanish ambassador informed the Pope of the Earls' arrival, 'He was dismayed, thinking he would have to support them, but as soon as he knew that they would receive help, he became more cheerful.' The ambassador's first encounter with the Irish did little to cheer him up. He had been instructed to pay O'Neill 400 ducats and the Earl of Tyrconnell 300 ducats 'but they showed such contempt for this amount that their majordomos, by orders of their masters, refused to accept it.' The Earls were so aggrieved that they threatened to leave immediately for Madrid. They demanded no less than 2,000 ducats a month each, a sum that was paid to Charles of Lorraine, Duke of Aumale. 'They have strong feelings on what is due to their blood and position and here in

Rome the eyes of the world were on them.' The ambassador would only give them 1,400 ducats between the two, presumably being 700 ducats for each of two months which was the original grant, which astonished them as 'it was not sufficient to cover a quarter of our necessary expenses and this would be very harmful to our reputation'. The money was paid from Naples and not always on time, which caused them more discomfort. 'Their misfortunes have done so little to humble them that they take it as an insult not to be given immediately all they demand.' O'Neill did not wish O'Donnell to know that he was receiving more in case it might cause bad blood between them. The ambassador admitted that they were in great want.

The Irish complained about their treatment directly to the King of Spain. 'Within our houses we live in such straitened circumstances that we would not wish anyone to know it. We cannot show ourselves in public, or pay a visit, under appearances that would befit even ordinary gentlemen.' Even the ambassador in Rome pleaded with the King to be more generous, claiming that Rome was a very expensive city but the King replied that the Irish 'have little cause for displeasure for everything possible has been done for them'. The Doge of Venice had been informed from Milan that O'Neill 'before leaving Ireland, which he did on the understanding with His Majesty that the King had told him to abandon all his property, and to come at once, for money would not be wanting, nor honourable entertainment, and confirmed these promises by letters-patent.'

The Spanish ambassador in London wrote to Philip III pointing out that while O'Neill was alive in Rome the English would always fear and for that reason that Spain would do 'well to keep that man satisfied'. 'Ireland is almost in a state of tumult and revolt and this would increase if they knew that Tyrone would return with help.' The ambassador was convinced 'that if this opportunity were lost by the Pope and the King of Spain it would never return in their lifetime'.

The King believed that the Pope should take a lead, with the co-operation of the Earls, in the affairs of Ireland. 'Ireland belongs to the Apostolic See from ancient times and this should be sufficient reason to move a generous Pontiff who would wish to leave a good name to posterity.'

Paul V, who became Pope just two years earlier, had already clashed with James I when the latter introduced an oath denouncing the papal claim to depose a ruler and the Pope condemned his action. He was very much a reforming Pope, though like many of his predecessors – including his immediate predecessor, Clement VIII, generally regarded as a Counter-Reformation Pope, who made two of his nephews cardinals – and some of his successors, he too was guilty of nepotism, making his nephew Scipione Borghese a cardinal. Scipione was responsible for building Villa Borghese with its spacious Giardino, now the largest recreational garden in Rome. The Pope's brother, Giovanni Battista Borghese, was made the governor of Castello Sant' Angelo as well as Prefetto of Rome, while he shared the profitable salt monopoly with another brother, Francesco. *La Famiglia*, no less than *la Mamma*, was and is central to Italian life, and popes, like others, were expected to advance the social status of their families which usually involved making nephews cardinals and arranging prestigious marriages for their nieces.

Pope
Paul V

Even in modern times when the brothers and sisters of the saintly John XXIII complained that he had done nothing for his family, he gently reminded them that he invited them every year to dine with him in the Vatican.

It is true that Clement showed great kindness and charity towards the poor, the sick and those imprisoned. But the Spanish ambassador's impression of a penny-pinching Paul V does not altogether match the reality or other views of the same Pope. Ó Cianáin estimated that the Pope was worth about fifty-four thousand pounds a year but added that 'the poverty and misery it relieves is huge and indescribable'. According to him, no less than ten thousand persons were supported by the papal purse including a group called 'the Pope's children', a term coined long before a modern Irish economic guru decided to use it to describe the generation who grew up in the aftermath of Pope John Paul II's visit to Ireland. The original group were orphans, four hundred and eighty-three in all, including boys and girls who were reared and supported by the Pope and provided with the best of education. Ó Cianáin saw them on Whit Monday march in procession, preceded by the papal guard, to St Peter's, where sixteen of the girls were married, with the Pope paying their dowry.

Paul V was credited with establishing a grain storehouse for the poor as well as restoring two aqueducts and erecting a number of fountains. As a result of this, and other Popes' actions, modern Rome has the finest public drinking water in the world. He was also responsible for the completion of the facade of St Peter's Basilica. He completed the Quirinale Palace in Monte Cavallo which was used as a papal summer house because of its elevation, and there he first received the Earls. It remained a papal residence until 1870 when Pio Nono was turfed out to make way for the King of Italy, Vittorio Emanuele II and in 1947 it became the residence of the President of Italy. On the world stage, Paul V was a fervent supporter of the Jesuit Reductions in Paraguay, introduced Chinese as a liturgical language, and the study of Latin, Greek and Hebrew into the newly founded seminaries. He donated numerous volumes to the Vatican Library and established the papal archives. He also promulgated the *Rituale Romanum*. He canonised Frances of Rome, at which ceremony the Irish party were present, and beatified Ignatius Loyola and Francis Xavier as well as Philip Neri and Teresa of Avila. On the negative side, it was on his watch that the heliocentric theories of Galileo Galilei of Pisa were condemned by the Congregation of the Index, and a member of that Congregation who led the condemnation, was Peter Lombard, the Archbishop of Armagh.

The Irish were received by the Pope on Sunday, 4 May, at three o'clock in the afternoon and the audience lasted about an hour. It took place at the Quirinale and the cardinals had provided them with coaches to convey them there. Then, as the custom was, 'they kissed with humility and reverence his holy foot' and took their leave after receiving the Pope's benediction. The English ambassador's prediction that all O'Neill could expect in Rome was 'bulls and benedictions' was beginning to ring true. More papal favours were to follow in the coming days and weeks. On the eve of Whit Sunday, they were invited to attend vespers in St Peter's where O'Neill was given a place of honour close to the Pope and opposite him.

On 29 May, the anniversary of the Pope's election, Cardinal Borghese sent one of his noblemen to invite them to St Peter's to attend a special Mass to honour the occasion and they were again given a place of honour. To enhance the occasion, Frances of Rome was canonised and the Pope's niece was despatched to fetch the Countess Catherine who was given precedence even over the Pope's own sisters. This occasion was reported to the English Secretary of State by the spy, James Rath, who continued to infiltrate with immunity the Irish party in Rome. To

Quirinale
Palace

disguise his identity in case of interception, Rath passed himself off as a
Catholic writing to another Catholic, even sending a picture of Saint
Frances, as well as forty *Agnus Deis*, and 'more if he had them'. The
evening before the canonisation, the Pope's niece took all the Irish ladies
to see the illumination of St Peter's and the fireworks in Sant' Angelo –
'the grandest that can be imagined.'

On Trinity Sunday, the Countess Catherine, Nuala O'Donnell, Bríd
O'Neill, Rose O'Dogherty and the other Irish ladies were given a special audience. The English ambassador in Venice commented that
O'Neill's wife was 'much commended and admired for her beauty and
modesty of behaviour' but added insultingly that O'Neill 'has done well
to bring her to Rome, in case all other means should shrink'. This was
O'Neill's second audience with the Pope, this time 'to present the
Countess, his wife, and the gentlewomen with her'. The ambassador
claimed that it was Peter Lombard, Archbishop of Armagh 'that doeth
all things for him, with certain other spiritual men he hath in his
company, and of his own country'.

Perhaps the greatest papal honour conferred on the Irish was when eight of their number were chosen to carry the canopy over the Blessed Sacrament borne by the Pope in procession on the feast of Corpus Christi. These probably included, besides O'Neill and O'Donnell, Hugh O'Neill, Baron of Dungannon, Caffar O'Donnell, Cuchonnacht Maguire and three others not easily identified. It was the first time that a single nationality was chosen for this task and the foreign ambassadors usually chosen on such an occasion, were 'jealous, envious and surprised'. But the spy Rath reported: 'Italians speak much good and very honourable of these Earls; and the Earls themselves keep their state gallantly. It seemed some good vein of gold as yet flows with full tide which he prays God may not soon fall to a low ebb.'

It was an imposing procession with a large number of the clergy, regular and secular, carrying a thousand lighted torches, followed by twenty-six archbishops and bishops, and thirty-six cardinals, then the Pope with the Irish canopy-bearers, flanked by the Swiss Guard. The Roman pontiffs had largely carried on the roles of the Caesars, their classical ancestors, as well as some of their better-known ploys such as 'bread and circuses' to keep their citizenry content. Impressive processions on the numerous feast days were a sort of religious expression of the earlier spectacle of gladiatorial contests in the Colosseum.

The feast of Corpus Christi was first established in Liège in Belgium in the middle of the thirteenth century to promote Eucharistic devotion. Later, it was adopted by Pope Urban IV, himself a Belgian, and Thomas Aquinas composed many of the texts associated with it, including the popular hymn, *Lauda Sion*. The procession came to be the hallmark of the feast for many local churches in the fourteenth century and greatly contributed to the popularity of the feast. The Eucharistic procession came to have great social and commercial significance, as well as an expression of popular religiosity. While the feast of Corpus Christi was known in Ireland – an Augustinian monastery in Benada, County Sligo and the first Observant monastery in Ireland, was dedicated to Corpus Christi early in the fifteenth century – as with so many other mainstream religious practices, the Corpus Christi procession did not become a feature of religious life in rural Ireland until the last years of the nineteenth century and did not become widespread until the early years of the twentieth.

All these papal privileges conferred on the Irish only served, whether he was aware of it or not, to reduce the 'great' O'Neill to the status of little more than a papal poodle and not even a pampered one at that, particularly in the eyes of English observers. Over the next while O'Neill undertook the pilgrimage of the seven churches of Rome: the Basilicas of San Pietro, Santa Maria Maggiore, San Giovanni in Laterno, Santa Croce in Gerusalemme, San Sebastiano, St Pauls Outside the Walls and St Lawrence Outside the Walls. The Pope gave instructions to have 'exhibited to them all the relics of each church to which they would go'.

Ostia   Grievous personal disasters awaited him just around the corner. In the middle of July, when the heat and humidity in Rome was oppressive and almost intolerable, the Earl of Tyrconnell, the Baron of Dungannon and Caffar O'Donnell, left Rome for a change of air at Ostia, where they spent two days and two nights. The priest, Doctor Donal O'Carroll, followed them. Ostia Antica was then surrounded by a very low-lying, mosquito-infested swamp at the mouth of the Tiber, a place described by Ó Cianáin as 'one of the worst and most unhealthy for climate in all Italy'. On their return to Rome Tyrconnell went down with 'a hot, fiery, violent fever', probably resulting from malaria. In the days that followed Caffar O'Donnell, the Baron of Dungannon and Donal O'Carroll caught the fever, as well as the page and footman who had accompanied them to Ostia. The Irish group were probably singularly

San Pietro in   unfitted to withstand such an infection. The Pope sent his own personal
Montorio   physician, but the Earl continued to decline and died eleven days later

on 28 July. He was only thirty-three years old. He was buried in a Franciscan habit in the monastery of San Pietro in Montorio, where his tomb can still be viewed today. San Pietro had a long Spanish connection going back to Ferdinand and Isabella. The Spanish royal family sponsored the decoration of the interior in the sixteenth and seventeenth centuries. The Four Masters later recorded his death: 'Sorrowful in the short life and early

eclipse of him who was there deceased, for he was a brave, protecting, valiant, puissant, and warlike man, and had often been in the gap of danger, along with his brother Hugh Roe in defence of his religion and his patrimony.'

With the subsequent death of Caffar, their grief-stricken sister Nuala was the soul survivor of the breed of Iníon Dubh, and the O'Donnell poet, Eoghan Rua Mac an Bhaird addressed his lament to her:

An dá chloich sin ós a gcoinn
dá bhfaicdís ógbhaidh Éirionn,
ar aoi a líneadh do léaghadh
caoi mhíleadh do mhoisgéaladh.

Those two stones above them –
If the young men of Ireland were to see them
And read the lines on them,
It would awake the cries of heroes ...

Níor léigsiod asteach na dtír
sect Lúitéir léighionn Cailbhín,
drong shaobh ré ar gheabhsad gigil,
ná maor easbog eithrigigh.

They did not allow into their land
The Lutheran sect, the teaching of Calvin,
Perverse folk against whom they took a loathing,
Nor governing heretical bishops.

Caffar's page, Muiris, died shortly afterwards. The Spanish ambassador informed the King of Tyrconnell's death and proposed that he would continue to pay his allowance to his dependants who were in great need: 'They have no protection or help at all except what they get from God and Your Majesty.' His Majesty readily agreed that the allowance should be continued but in great secrecy and that they should continue to remain in Rome. O'Neill also wrote to Philip III informing him of Tyrconnell's death and the imminent death of Caffar, and asked him to help Caffar's wife, Rose O'Dogherty, as well as Tyrconnell's sister, Nuala, who wanted to go to Flanders. O'Neill made a special appeal for the King's protection of Hugh O'Donnell, the infant Earl of Tyrconnell, whom they had left in Louvain. The ambassador also tried to have O'Neill's allowance increased, which was barely enough for food, and in other respects they suffered great want:

> They are so poor that one must have compassion for them. The Pope gives them a house but not one stick of furniture and they have neither beds nor chairs. The unfortunates have not money to buy such bare necessities and, as there are many Irish with the Earl, a large sum would be necessary to buy even what would be needed so that they might not be forced to sleep on the floors.

It was not unusual to provide people with unfurnished accommodation. The Irish students in Collège des Lombards in Paris later in that century were each given a room but were expected to provide their own bed, desk and chair, which they sold off when their term was ended. Presumably, the Persian ambassador, who had previously occupied Palazzo dei Penitenzieri, took his furniture with him when he left.

The English received a similar account of the poor condition of the Irish. 'It is written from Rome that Tyrone and his company are very much discouraged to find that the spiritual and temporal treasure of the church produces nothing more in their favour than a good welcome and the entertainment they receive ...' O'Neill's allowance must have been increased in September when the Spanish ambassador reported that he 'shows no more discontentment'.

The King of England was also informed of Tyrconnell's death which was blamed on 'a riotous journey which they took to Ostia'. The death was confirmed by the appearance in Rome in mourning by one of his followers who 'walks now these streets (in black weeds) in fashion of a grandee, followed by two pages, and accompanied by four other of his countrymen in the like attire.' The report added rather bitchily that the clothes must have been provided by their hosts, 'for what they brought hither would hardly defray the charge of their tailors'.

Donal O'Carroll died on 8 August. He was from Tipperary and studied at the Irish College in Lisbon, which was run by the Jesuits, where he acquired a doctorate in theology. He was for six years vicar-general of Killaloe and was deputed by the Munster clergy to go to Rome to inform the Pope of the dire state of the Irish church. There he became the procurator of the Irish clergy. He was probably a member of the Jesuits and was described as such by the English who also labelled him 'the firebrand of Limerick'.

The Baron of Dungannon and Caffar O'Donnell were moved to another palace on Monte Citorio but Caffar died in the middle of September and was buried with his brother in San Pietro in Montorio.

The Corpus Christi procession was Maguire's last official appearance in Rome and he left two days later for Naples which was then a dependency of Spain. He may have been sent by O'Neill to promote the idea of another expedition to Ireland or there may have been simply a more personal reason as the Spanish ambassador had refused to give him any financial help. He had approached the Spanish ambassador at the end of May, who duly reported the encounter to Madrid. 'There is another noble with them, called Maguire, who is very important in his own country. He says that he had done great service in Ireland for Your Majesty and that he has lost great estates. He wishes that Your Majesty give him a grant.' Maguire, and MacGowan who had accompanied him to Naples, were seized with 'a wild and raging, painful and harmful fever' and after seven weeks there they had set out for Genoa where they died on 12 August 1608. They were buried in the Franciscan monastery in the city, in the habit of that Order. The Four Masters described Maguire as an 'intelligent, comely, courageous, magnanimous, rapid-marching, adventurous man, endowed with wisdom, personal beauty, and all the other good qualifications'.

Ó Cianáin recorded these tragic deaths as he best knew how as a trained Irish annalist: 'It may well be believed that it was not through good fortune or the best of fate that it happened to Ireland that so many of the choicest of the descendants of Míl Easpáinne died suddenly, one after another, in a foreign and strange land, far removed from their native land.' Ó Cianáin followed the generally accepted view then, both in Ireland and in Spain, that the Irish were descendant from Spanish invaders who settled in Ireland and, interestingly, the Irish in Spain, both students and others, unlike the English Catholics there, were given Spanish nationality.

Ó Cianáin's last entry is dated 20 November 1608 and it has no reference to the Irish. It is a lengthy and colourful description of the spectacular entry of the Duke of Nevers, ambassador extraordinary of his Most Christian Majesty, Henry IV of France, to the Pope. It was a live baroque performance which could hardly be as well choreographed today by a major Hollywood studio. It is probably Ó Cianáin's best piece of writing. The Duke entered by the gate of Sant' Angelo close to Saint Peter's. The entry of the Earls into Rome pales into insignificance compared to this spectacle:

'There were three-score mules drawing their carriages at the head of the procession, wherein was his livery, his plate and his valuables, and upon their heads, were grand, variegated, particoloured embroidered clothing, with conspicuous combs. After these there were twelve mules carrying beautiful, short, painted trunks, and on each mule there was a sheet of red velvet adorned with gold and silver thread, and the coat of arms of the Duke himself skilfully wrought on each sheet. On each mule there were very broad, strong blinkers and they were all made of pure bright, refined silver. The long hooks, and all the buckles and nails of their bridles were likewise made of silver. There were tall plumes, with a variety of all colours, standing on the heads of the mules. Long, stout reins of red silk, having large tassels at their ends, were attached to the bridle of each mule ... The cardinal's own mules, to the number of about forty, with red footcloths came after these, and on each of them rode a cardinal's servant. Next there were a trio of noblemen and a trio of trumpeters. After these came the footmen of the Duke himself in grand livery, twenty in number, and riding on horses. After these were the Duke's pages, twelve in number, and their dress was of yellow velvet. After these were the Romans, about two hundred great noblemen, riding on beautiful mettlesome horses, and dressed in black. Next were the Frenchmen, eighty horsemen on beautiful active, swift, well-equipped horses, with many golden chains about their necks. Forty barons and lords came next, two and two, and they were as stately as the Frenchmen, but their dress was of dark colour. After these were four of the Pope's trumpeters, and four drummers belonging to the Romans. They wore red glittering suits. After them were sixty men of the officers and servants of the Pope on horseback. They and their horses were dressed in red. After them was a large group of the nobles of the Romans. After these were four great noblemen of the chief country of the King of Spain, dressed in black. Next to them were twenty titled noblemen, and they were from France. Precious, grand and valuable were their dress and their horses. After these came the Duke of Force (a famous French general), with a great group of horsemen, dukes and princes of Rome and of the rest of Italy. The Duke of Force came with the greatest of splendour and grandeur in all the world. After these came the Pope's brother, with the Pope's Swiss Guard about him. In front of him on the road there were four horsemen in red suits with great maces of pure bright silver. Next came twelve lackeys of the Duke's party and six Swiss in suits of yellow. Following them were two coloured men, their garments made of red damask, with much wide, golden laces. Near them was a team of beautiful horses, with saddles of red velvet covered with embroidery in golden thread. The Duke himself came next, riding on a beautiful, white, small, stout horse, a footcloth of Indian velvet, covered with golden laces, upon his saddle. The long strong hooks of the bridle, its buckles, the stirrups of the saddle, and all its parts, were made of red gold. About himself was a splendid, valuable garment, all embroidered with golden thread. There were many diamonds and precious stones united in the cord of his hat on his head, and his hand was continually in motion doffing his hat while saluting and bowing to those who saw and welcomed him. The Patriarch of Jerusalem was on his right hand, the Archbishop of Volterra on his left. After him was Monsignor de Breves, the ambassador in ordinary of the King of France in the city. After these were fifty bishops and grand prelates of the church, each riding on a beautiful mule, with the most excellent saddles and footcloths.

Except for a brief note added a year later, this was Ó Cianáin's swansong. His manuscript was later deposited in the Irish Franciscan college of St Isidore's in Rome where it lay until 1872 when it was transferred to Merchants' Quay, Dublin and a bilingual version of it was finally published in 1916, just in time to greet the Easter Rising.

Chapter Eleven

Last Days

THE ENGLISH AMBASSADOR IN Venice reported in October: 'Tyrone's son continues sick of that distemperature which he took in company of Tyrconnell and his brother at Ostia, who as he has formerly signified, are both dead, as also Macguier and his companion at Genoa, while they attended passage for Spain.' Ó Cianáin made one short addendum to record the death of O'Neill's son, Hugh, the Baron of Dungannon on 23 September 1809, at the age of twenty-four:

Och! Och! Chráigh agus threaghd bás Aodha ár gcroí!

Mo chreach Aodha.

Och! Och! The death of Hugh has broken and pierced our heart.

Woe is me, Hugh!

His old master, the Franciscan Aodh Mac Aingil, wrote a commemorative verse about him:

A fhir fhéachas an cnáimh
Ná fiafraigh de chách cé hé,
Ná bí in ainbhios, druid liom –
Mise ceann Aodh Uí Néill.
Cuimhnigh an bhreith a rug orm,
Leanfaidh sibhse ár lorg 's ár ré,
Ní fhuil de dhifir ann súd

Ach sibhse inniu 's sinne inné
To the man who looks at these bones
Don't ask anyone who he is,
Don't be ignorant, come close
I am the head of Hugh O'Neill.
Remember the fate that befell me,
You will follow our tracks and our era,
There is no difference there
Except you today and us yesterday.

He was buried like his uncles in San Pietro in Montorio and the Spanish ambassador gave the Earl 400 crowns to defray the funeral expenses. There is a lengthy Latin inscription on his tomb which ended with 'his untimely death destroyed the hope that everyone placed in him, because of his outstanding qualities of mind and body, that some day he would make the Catholic faith flourish again in that country.' Mac an Bhaird described him as 'a prince in look, in deed and word', and he lamented him with his two uncles:

Dá mhac rígh don fhréimh sin Chuin
atá ar gach taobh d'Ó Domhnuill –
na trí cuirp ré síneann sibh
fír-earr ár n-uilc a n-oidhidh!

Two king's sons of Conn's line
Are on either side of O'Donnell –
The three bodies by which you lie –
Their death is the very end of evil !

O, had these twain, and he, the third,
The Lord of Mourne, O'Niall's son,
Three royal youths alas are gone,
who lived for Erin's weal, but died for Erin's woe,

Ah! could the men of Ireland read
The names these note-less burial-stones display to view,
Their wounded hearts afresh would bleed,
Their tears gush forth again, their groans resound anew.

The Baron and his two uncles were not the first Irish royal burials in Rome. Almost five and a half centuries previously Donough O'Brien, son of Brian Ború, was buried in the church of San Stefano Rotundo.

Nuala O'Donnell and her sister-in-law, Rose O'Dogherty, wished to return to Flanders, where the infant son of Rory as well as Rose's son

Tomb of
Donough
O'Brien in
San Stefano
Rotundo

had remained, and O'Neill wrote to Spain on their behalf requesting money for the journey, as well as a subsistence allowance for them when they arrived there. She was suffering from bad health in Rome. Surprisingly, the King, while granting Nuala an allowance, would not countenance her going to Flanders: 'They must not leave Rome, for they are better there than anywhere else.' Finally, at the end of August 1610, the King acceded to her request, 'provided none of her kinsmen or any other Irish in Rome go with her,' so that the King of England had no cause for complaint. It was September 1611 before she finally left and she was given three hundred crowns for the journey. Rose O'Dogherty had even more difficulty making it to Flanders. Like Nuala, she sought permission in September 1608. Almost three and a half years later she was still in Rome and the King ordered his ambassador there to 'calm her and divert her from this purpose' but it was too late. She had already left, having received from the ambassador three hundred crowns for the journey and eighty crowns a month subsistence allowance in Flanders.

O'Neill too wanted to go to Flanders and approached the Spanish ambassador on the night of 11 November 1608 'in great secrecy' to make his request. He wanted to be 'nearer to the Irish Catholics, better able to correspond with them and so help them not lose their way'. He was obsessed by the 'pernicious climate' in Rome and that his life was endangered by the 'great heat'. The ambassador also pleaded his cause with the King, 'in view of his age, his poor health, and the fact that many of his family have died because this climate is so adverse to them'. The answer from Spain was always the same. 'Wherever the Earl might go, it would displease the King of England; therefore he should be advised to remain where he is.' The King told his ambassador: 'You will console him and calm him with the good words you will know how to use, and I will always have due consideration for his person and for anything which concerns him.'

News of events in Ireland were causing O'Neill considerable alarm, particularly the plans for planting Ulster with colonists. The idea had been mooted as early as September 1607 when Sir Geoffrey Fenton in Ireland suggested to the English Secretary of State, 'what a door is opened to the King not only to pull down forever these two proud houses of O'Neill and O'Donnell but also to bring in colonies of the English to plant both counties'. At the end of October 1608 the Venetian ambassador reported: 'They have resolved to confiscate Tyrone's property and that of the other rebels.' Part of the proceeds would go to the King and part to some Irish 'to secure their hostility to Tyrone and other rebels ...' According to the ambassador, 'the King ... has shown those people what they did not understand before ... that they were tyrannised by the Tyrones and other chiefs.' In January 1609 King James issued orders for the plantation of the lands of O'Neill and O'Donnell and their followers among English and Scots settlers and the conditions for the plantation were printed. Florence Conry received a copy and immediately sent a Spanish translation of it to the Spanish Council of State.

Plantation of Ulster

Philip, through his ambassador in Rome, gave O'Neill permission to negotiate a reconciliation with the King of England. O'Neill was 'greatly distressed at such a belated and discouraging reply', pointing out that had he received it at any time during the years following his departure from Ireland, it might have been possible to achieve a reconciliation with King James who was then anxious for it. 'The least your Majesty must do is to procure without delay that the King of England return his lands and admit him to favour.' He urged him to send a letter immediately to his ambassador in London to negotiate a reconciliation with the King, before English and Scottish planters settled on the lands and the inhabitants were banished.

There is some evidence that King James's attitude to O'Neill may have mellowed somewhat. In a conversation with the Venetian ambassador in the summer of 1609 the King had told him that 'the Earl is an old man of sixty-five and could not live much longer,' and added 'that he had never given Tyrone any occasion for disgust. When in London he was highly humoured and had been out hunting with the King.' These may have been another reason for the King's change of heart. His Secretary of State had just been informed that the Pope had conferred the title of King of Ireland on O'Neill, which, in fact, was not true.

Meanwhile in Ireland there were rumours of O'Neill's imminent return, which deterred some of the Scots and English planters from settling on the confiscated lands of the Earls: 'Their fear of him gnaws at their entrails.' King James was forced to cut short a tour of his kingdom because there was a 'rumour that Tyrone is going back to Ireland and that, in view of this, a son of his, who is an excellent soldier at present serving the Archduke with a regiment of infantry, is to move to Flanders.' The Venetian ambassador thought that the introduction of Protestant planters would be 'greatly abhorred by the Irish' who were 'by nature deeply devoted to the Apostolic See … and would be very glad to hear the name of Spain in Ireland, where the opinion is held that the Spanish are the only nation that truly defends the Catholic Faith'.

Much to the fury of O'Neill, Philip procrastinated and delayed making a decision and he complained bitterly early in 1611 to the Spanish ambassador that in spite of all his letters, he still had not received a clear reply. 'This has been the cause of his ruin, for the King of England has seen what little account His Majesty has made of the Earl and the delay that has been made of the settlement of his affairs; consequently the English King has given his estates to Englishmen and Scots. Had the Earl believed that this were to happen he would have delivered himself unto his King rather than come to such a pass. Indeed he is not beyond doing this, or anything else that may suit him, if there should be any further delay in dealing with his affairs.' The Plantation was already under way by the end of April 1610 and O'Neill was quick to realise that, once carried out, the Plantation would be irreversible as he impressed upon the Spanish ambassador, 'for the King is distributing the lands of the country among heretics and once they are rooted there, it will be difficult to remove them'. Time has shown his words to have been prophetic. He wrote himself to the King: 'I can be of more service to Your Majesty in my own country or anywhere else than here in Rome where I can only bury my bones with those of the other Irish who have died here.' The Four Masters, with the benefit of hindsight, saw the Plantation as a direct consequence of the Flight: 'It was indeed from the departure of the Earls that it came to pass that their principalities, their territories, their estates, their lands, their forts, their fruitful harbours, their fishful bays, were taken from the Irish of the province of Ulster and given in their presence to foreign tribes: and they were expelled and banished into other countries, where most of them died.'

England was worried that the Plantation might provoke O'Neill to some desperate action as the Venetian ambassador reported from London: 'The King is watching the movements of the Earl of Tyrone, as he holds it certain that the present conjuncture of affairs will tempt the Pope to some of his old designs. I have this from a very sure source.' The Spanish ambassador in London also believed the time was ripe for action in Ireland as the situation there was 'such that we may promise ourselves the best of results if His Holiness should wish to send Tyrone to Ireland ... and that if this opportunity was lost by the Pope and the King of Spain, it would never return in their lifetime.' Philip asked his ambassador to sound out the Pope and, when he did, he reported back: 'It is very clear to me that we can expect no financial aid from him.'

O'Neill sent Conry to Spain and also his son, Henry, from Flanders to join him there while O'Neill's own envoy, Matthew Tully had been there already for over a year. Conry presented the King with O'Neill's memorial, begging him to take measures to prevent the confiscations of O'Neill's lands. Conry pointed out that the most effective means to achieve this was for the King to send an army to Ireland, consisting at least in part of the 1,500 men of the Irish regiment in Flanders, and all this could be done in the name of the Pope who should contribute financially. 'This help would be sufficient to take Ireland with speed.' The King was not persuaded and it would be a 'rash undertaking', and using the Pope as a cover would not fool the King of England.

While O'Neill was busy pressing his claims on Philip, he suffered a more tragic and personal loss than that of his confiscated estates in Ireland. His second son, Henry, died in Spain after a short illness, on 25 August 1610. He was only twenty-three years old and the last of the brood of Siobhán O'Donnell.

The question of who should succeed him as colonel of the Irish Regiment in Flanders was immediately raised. Florence Conry proposed Owen Roe O'Neill, a nephew of Hugh, the son of a younger brother, and who had accompanied Henry to Spain, 'for there is no other suitable person of his blood in Flanders'. The Archduke's government proposed John O'Neill, Hugh's eldest son by Catherine Magennis, who had been left in Louvain and was now fourteen years old. 'It is thought that the appointment of his son would give more pleasure and consolation to the good old man than that of any other person.' It was in fact O'Neill's wish also, as the Spanish ambassador reported to Spain: 'The affection which all the soldiers had for the late Colonel and the honour and respect they owe to the Earl his father, give reason to hope that all will be well pleased to serve Your Majesty under his command.' As he was too young and had no military experience, it was proposed that a major be appointed to lead the regiment in the meantime. Florence Conry recommended that Owen Roe O'Neill should be appointed major and this was done. John O'Neill was a page to the Infanta Isabella and was still pursuing his studies. O'Neill was not averse to capitalising on the sympathy evoked in Spain following the death of Henry and he asked Philip III to make John a knight commander of Calatrava which included an income from the commandery. The Infanta Isabella also wrote strongly supporting the request and the King agreed.

He had previously asked Philip to sponsor his other son, Brian at his confirmation. Not wishing to offend the King of England, the King instructed his ambassador in Brussels to act as sponsor and the Archduke Albert nominated a Spanish grandee to act as sponsor in his place. He was confirmed by the Archbishop of Malines and he took the names of Philip and Albert after which the ambassador gave him a chain worth a hundred ducats and entertained him to a banquet. He was admitted as a page at the Archduke's court where he assumed the name Philip, after his royal godfather. Five years later, when he was only eleven, he came to a tragic end. He was found hanging in his lodgings in Brussels after he returned from school. The Spanish ambassador ruled out suicide as 'the boy was so well-disposed and was such a good Christian'. He suspected that he had been strangled and afterwards hanged to hide the fact. Brian O'Neill was buried in an unmarked grave in St Anthony's. This was one tragedy that O'Neill was not burdened with as he had just predeceased his youngest son.

His other son by Catherine Maginnis, Conn, had been captured by Sir Toby Caulfield and kept in his house in Charlemont for a number of years. Later he was taken to Dublin and sent to Trinity College 'where they send the first-born sons of the most Catholic Irish gentlemen to be educated in the sect of Calvin'. When O'Neill heard of it he wrote angrily: 'A son of mine is even now being reared in heresy, but I trust in God that the blood in his veins will not permit such a deception and that one day he will avenge this outrage for me.' Later, on the orders of James I, he was sent over to England where he was sent to Eton College. Finally, he was committed to the Tower of London in 1622 and nothing further was heard of him.

Meanwhile, negotiations had started in Madrid regarding a marriage between Philip's daughter, Infanta Dona Maria and James's eldest son, Henry, Prince of Wales. When O'Neill learned of this he impressed on the ambassador that, in the event of this marriage, the agreement should include the restoration of the Earl's estate and liberty of conscience. When Henry died in November 1612, his brother Charles became Prince of Wales and the negotiations continued.

In the summer of 1613 a surprising development took place in Louvain where the English made an approach to the Irish Franciscans there, indicating they were eager for a reconciliation with O'Neill. The

English
Overture

Guardian of St Anthony's, Aodh MacAingil, who had been tutor to the deceased O'Neill brothers, wrote immediately to Hugh in Rome. He had been approached by an English agent, sent by Viscount Rochester, who was then a favourite of James I, and who 'on behalf of His Majesty, promises that the terms of agreement will not be so rigorous as they were when in your hand you held a naked sword, for the King will give you either your own lands or the equivalent or even better lands.' The agent urged that 'the opportunity and the time is now or never.' What prompted James to make this overture to O'Neill at this juncture is not certain. It may have been a pathological fear of him, as the ambassador in Madrid had earlier suggested: 'If the Earl of Tyrone came from Rome with three-hundred men, or even alone, it would be very easy to

Aodh MacAingil. Mural, St Isidore's, Rome

conquer all Ireland, for if the Earl called upon the people and they knew he was coming, they would rise up and seize power of the whole king-dom of Ireland.' The country was alive with rumours, fed to the people by wandering friars, who had returned from the continent. One of them, Turlough MacCroddyn, 'lately come from overseas', said Mass that summer in a glen somewhere between Tyrone and Fermanagh. 'Tyrone was coming with 18,000 men sent by the King of Spain,' he told his enraptured congregation, 'and that according to a prophesy in a book at Rome, England had only two more years to rule in Ireland.' The President of Munster warned that O'Neill's arrival in Ireland would be sufficient 'to disturb the realm and to set fire in every part thereof and the natives' swords will be in our throats in every part of the realm, like the Sicilian Vespers before the clouds of mischief should appear.'

O'Neill informed Philip III of the English overture, telling him that 'he does not wish to take any decision or to agree to any reconciliation with the said King, unless it be with the consent and on the order of Your Catholic Majesty.' The matter was discussed by the Spanish Council of State in Madrid and the unanimous opinion was that O'Neill should not pursue the matter as the English King could not be trusted. Philip accepted their recommendation and wrote to his ambassador to advise O'Neill to consider well the risk he would be taking. O'Neill sent another memorial to the King, written in the third person as was customary, pointing out that 'considering the age that is upon him, the delay of help from Spain, the continuous danger to his life, not only because of his circumstances, but also because of the climate of this land where his sons and vassals who came with him have perished ... all he needs is His Catholic Majesty's permission to go to Flanders where he may carry out the negotiations and correspond more easily with his vassals as with the Council of England pending the settlement of his affairs.' He also asked that a few others, notably Seán MacDavitt and the Tyrconnell poet, Eóghan Mac an Bhaird, be allowed to accompany him. But it was too late. King James was no longer interested in reconciliation, as the Spanish ambassador reported to Madrid. The new Spanish ambassador in London, unlike his predecessors, was in favour of a policy of appeasement to improve the situation of Catholics in Ireland. Philip instructed his ambassador in Rome to tell the Pope that it would be advisable not to allow Tyrone leave Rome. 'Neither should His Holiness give ear to any new plans which may be suggested to him over there.' Not that Paul v was likely to.

At the very end of his biography, Seán O'Faolain wrote of O'Neill: 'Then, settled into his house in Rome, secure in the modest comfort of a Papal and Spanish pension, he gradually became just like any other distinguished emigré habituated to melancholy and homelessness and the routine of idle days.' Worse was to follow on the next page. His description of O'Neill as a 'tipsy old man' could not be further from the truth. And then he winds up his story with: 'The Earl sits alone with his glass – he drinks far too much nowadays – in no haste to go to bed since there is so little reason why he should rise betimes ... As the old drunken man sobs in his rage and misery, the glass tumbles, the wine slowly spills across the historian's page a long red streak of blood.'

Such a description is pure fiction, but then O'Faolain did not have the benefit of consulting the enormous number of documents covering these last years of O'Neill, which were later brought to light from the Spanish archives in Simancas. Between December 1607 and the year of his death, 1616, O'Neill sent no less than twenty-five letters or memorials to King Philip. The early ones were signed conjointly by himself and

Petition dated Louvain, 28 February 1608 to Philip III on behalf of the Irish College, Douai signed by Tyrone and Tyrconnell

Rory O'Donnell, but after the latter's sudden death in the summer of 1608, O'Neill continued to bombard Madrid with his appeals with fifteen letters or memorials. But these only represented a small proportion of his communications with Madrid. The greater amount were transmitted in the diplomatic bag by the Spanish ambassador. 'He goes often to the ambassador's house,' an English spy, who had spent two months either visiting daily or lodging in the O'Neill residence, reported to London in the autumn of 1615. Many of his interventions were on behalf of others such as Con O Conor Faly, Captain David Nelis, Seán Mac Davitt, the poet Eoghan Ruadh Mac an Bhaird, William Meade, Edmund Maginnis, brother of the Countess, the Scottish chieftain, Donough MacDonnell, Captain John Rath, and the Irish Regiment in Flanders.

His last letter to King Philip, on 7 January 1616, was an appeal on behalf of Pedro Blanco, who was among the Spaniards of the Armada shipwrecked off the Irish coast in 1588, found refuge with O'Neill and remained there for twenty years where he married and fathered a family. He particularly distinguished himself in the Battle of the Yellow Ford in 1598 and again took part in the Battle of Kinsale in 1603. 'At that time there was no other but this great soldier whom I could trust nor who would dare to take my letters across the enemy lines. At night he passed with great difficulty over the enemy trenches, and reached the town where the said Don Juan del Áquila was besieged, gave him my letters and brought back the replies with great care and loyalty.' O'Neill asked that Blanco be given 'some appointment near my person'.

In the autumn of 1615 a visitor arrived at the Salviati palace. Thomas Doyne, alias George White, was an English medical doctor and he was particularly welcome as the Countess was then ill and her Italian doctor 'could do her no good'. Whatever Doyne did for her, she became better and better. As a result he spent two months in the O'Neill household and even attended O'Neill himself, drawing blood from his legs. Bleeding a patient then was widely practised even for minor ailments and Doyne nowhere suggests that O'Neill was seriously ill. *Au contraire*, he describes an incident one evening which suggests O'Neill was in robust health or, as he put it, 'He is lusty and strong and well able to travel.'

O'Neill and his company were discussing England and Ireland and during the conversation, O'Neill drew his sword: 'His Majesty,' said he, 'thinks that I am not strong. I would he that hates me most in England were with me to see whether I am strong or no.' The others said: 'We would we were with forty thousand pounds in Ireland, to see what we should do.' Whereon Tyrone remarked: 'If I be not in Ireland within these two years, I will never desire more to look for it.' Doyne, who was an English spy as well as a medical doctor, also pointed out that there was a considerable amount of information passing to and from Ireland, especially through the Franciscan friars in Louvain. 'There is but few things done in the court of Ireland, let it be ever so secret, but it will be heard or else sought out by them.' English agents liked to refer to them as the 'machiavellian friars'.

Whatever good Doyne did for Countess Catherine, it did not last very long. On 9 January 1616, the Spanish ambassador on behalf of O'Neill asked the King for permission for his wife to travel to Flanders as the Italian climate was adversely affecting her health. He also requested that she should be given sufficient money so that she could 'travel in all comfort, with a sufficient escort and in a manner suited to her quality'. This was to be his last request and, like so many others, it was refused, the King suggesting that she might be better off to go to Naples or Sicily.

From the beginning of February 1615 to early January 1616, six months before he died, there were no less than ten dispatches from the Spanish ambassador to King Philip regarding O'Neill. On 15 March of that year he said 'that rather than live in Rome, he would prefer to go to his land with a hundred soldiers and die there in defence of the Catholic faith and of his fatherland.'

The Irish parliament, deliberately packed for the purpose, passed a bill in October 1614 for the attainder of O'Neill and O'Donnell and for the confiscation of their lands, and when the news reached Rome O'Neill was aroused to make another desperate attempt to return to Ireland with military support. He wrote to a member of the Spanish Council of State underlining the urgency of military aid and declared: 'We are resolved, those of us alive today, that we shall not wait to see the shameful day when the English completely conquer our provinces, profane our temples and seduce our children to their service. With our lives we shall procure the remedy for now, with the knife at our throats, to delay would be the surest misfortune. We are resolved to meet death with sword in hand.' He detailed the help that was required. Firstly, all the Irish soldiers, from himself down, in the Spanish service, particularly the Irish regiment in Flanders, should return to Ireland. Spain should provide them with munitions and arms and some money, fifty thousand ducats at the very least. He also sent letters to Florence Conry to be delivered to the Spanish ministers.

Conry consulted a Councillor of State in Madrid and he advised him not to continue to Valladolid where the court were then in residence, 'for the ambassador of England is never off guard and gets excited for the slightest reason'. Instead, the Councillor offered to present their case himself to one of the top Spanish ministers. 'The cause is worthy,' he informed the minister in July 1615, 'and I see the Irish determined in their purpose, for already from Rome they have sent several persons to raise the people through the intermediary of the priests of their nation.' He believed the Earl of Tyrone would leave Rome shortly for Genoa where, in disguise, he would await the Spanish King's answer and then embark on a ship which an Irish merchant was holding in readiness. They hoped to be in Ireland for St Michael's day when all the English magistrates were appointed. The matter was discussed at the end of that month by the Council of State and they took the view that this was not the time to have trouble with the King of England when Spain was trying to establish good relations with him as 'he appears to desire'. The King as usual agreed with his Council of State.

This final rejection of O'Neill's plan made no difference to O'Neill for whom God had other plans and, perhaps, other victories. He died in July 1616 after 'gaining the victory over the world and the Devil' as the Four Masters put it. 'Although he died far from Armagh, the burial place of his ancestors, it was a token that God was pleased with his life that the Lord permitted him no worse burial place, namely Rome, the head city of the Christians.' He was buried in San Pietro in Montorio beside his eldest son, Hugh and his brothers-in-law, Rory and Caffar O'Donnell. The simple inscription on his tomb – (Here lies) the bones

Tomb of Hugh
O'Neill in San
Pietro in
Montorio

Tomb of Hugh O'Neill in San Pietro in Montorio

of Prince Hugh O'Neill – is in stark contrast to the long and flowery obituaries on the two neighbouring tombs which were most probably composed by O'Neill himself. It strongly suggests that there was nobody of importance left in the Irish community in Rome who could be entrusted with this task. He had already fallen out with Peter Lombard.

Eoghan Rua Mac an Bhaird, who remained in Rome for almost another decade, (he died in 1635 and was buried in the cloister of St Anthony's in Louvain), could now complete his lament:

What do I say? Ah, woe is me.

Already we bewail in vain

Their fatal fall!

And Erin, once the great and free,

Now vainly mourns her breakless chain,

And iron thrall!

Then, daughter of O'Donnell! dry

Thine overflowing eyes and turn

Thy heart aside.

For Adam's race is born to die

And sternly the sepulchral urn

Mocks human pride.

But the *focail scoir*, the last words, like the first, with their benefit of hindsight, belong to the Four Masters:

Woe to the heart that meditated,

Woe to the mind that conceived,

Woe to the council that decided on

the project of their setting out on this voyage,

without knowing whether they should ever return

to their native principalities and patrimonies

to the end of the world.

Ireland would never be the same again. A new tradition took root beside the older Gaelic stock. It was eventually to express itself in a second state, Northern Ireland, in the island of Ireland.

Hugh O'Neill was a complex man and it is not easy either to assess the role he played in Irish history or to estimate his legacy. Later nineteenth-century nationalists liked to trace their roots from, and people their pantheon with, heroes like the legendary Cúchulainn, down to Brian Boru and Red Hugh O'Donnell to the iconic Wolfe Tone, whose name would have been unknown until long after his death to what was then an Irish-speaking population. When Tone went to France after the French Revolution, the Irish he met there were the remnants of the Irish colleges and regiments, to whom he took an almost instant dislike, often calling them 'blockheads' and condescendingly referring to their country cousins in Ireland as 'Pats'. One of these was General Henry Clarke, Napoleon's Minister of War, and the others, who spoke French perfectly and had been schooled in the university of revolution, were highly estimated by the French.

The 'great' O'Neill sits easily with such company, though he himself would probably never have claimed such a distinction. It is revealing to note that when he drew up his conditions for a reconciliation with James I, he limited his demand for freedom of conscience to the provinces of Ulster and Connacht. Provincialism, rather than nationalism, prevailed at that time and for a long time later. Many of the Irish colleges were reserved for students of a particular province, such as Lille, founded by Nugent in 1610, reserved exclusively for students from Meath and Leinster, as was Antwerp, which O'Neill visited, by Laurence Sedgrave for Leinstermen. Alcalá was founded for Munstermen alone while Bordeaux and Toulouse were preponderantly associated with Munster dioceses. Florence Conry complained that students from Connacht and Ulster were excluded from the Irish College in Salamanca. Even Collège des Lombards in Paris, which claimed to be an all-Ireland institution, had four superiors, one for each province, elected by the students of each province, right up to last decades of the eighteenth century.

As a champion of the Counter-Reformation, O'Neill finally grew into the role, particularly after his eight years in Italy. Who could not have been moved by the pomp and splendour of renaissance Rome, with Michaelangelo's painting of the ceiling of the Sistine Chapel, *The Creation of the World*, and his impressive sculpture of Moses seated, which adorns the tomb of Pope Julius II? He was also responsible for the magnificent cupola which crowned the newly built St Peter's Basilica. Leonardo da Vinci was a truly renaissance man who excelled as a sculptor, an architect, a painter, a student of anatomy and an engineer. His great masterpiece was an oil painting, *The Last Supper*, showing the reaction of the Apostles to Christ's statement that one of them was about to betray him. Raphael painted philosophical and historical subjects in the Vatican, but he is probably best known for his series of madonnas, which still dominate representation of Our Lady to the present day. O'Neill would have seen his oil-painting of the Transfiguration when he visited his son's tomb in San Pietro in Montorio. And then there were the spectacular parades and processions, like the entry of the French ambassador so beautifully described by Ó Cianáin in his last entry in his diary of the Flight. But above all, O'Neill had no choice but to play the Catholic card in his dealings with His Most Catholic Majesty, Philip III of Spain. He frequently invokes the Catholic faith as the reason for seeking Spanish aid. 'I wish to show clearly,' he wrote in 1612, 'that I do not seek my own interest but what is of greater service to God and to His Catholic Majesty.' And all his subsequent appeals were peppered with similar religious sentiments. Peter Lombard, who came to know O'Neill well in his later years, best sums up his religious motives:

'O'Neill had begun the war to protect his inheritance and had only subsequently taken on the mantle of a religious warrior.'

O'Faolain described O'Neill as 'a European figure in his intelligent awareness of the large nature of the conflict in which he took part.' Perhaps his is the best assessment of O'Neill's legacy:

> Fortunately for his country, however, he associated his struggle for independence with the whole movement of the Counter-Reformation, and that was a European idea and a European link, and it gave his people access to a great heritage and culture from which the principle of development has never been absent. And whether or not they have exploited that heritage to the full, so enlarging and fructifying, so colourful, so rich in urbanity and tolerance and discipline, and even in the hoary wisdom of the world, he did at any rate spin them that thread, and he did colour all future nationalism with its purple and gold. Had he not done so, that old Gaelic world would have died like the Incas and left behind gifts only to the antiquary and the philologist.

Perhaps, this is why he entitled his perceptive biography *The Great O'Neill*.